PRAISE FOR *W.*

"In this narrative, Lane seeks an origin s
are available and wondering about the legacy she is passing on. . . .
A multitangled exploration of family trauma and the forging of an
identity."

— *KIRKUS REVIEWS*

"In this evocative memoir, Cassandra Lane deftly uses the act of imagination to reclaim her ancestors' story as a backdrop for telling her
own. She renders each interior life with such tenderness and toughness that the tradition of Black women's storytelling leaps forward
within these pages—into fresh, daring, and excitingly new territory.
Lane's compelling voice couldn't be more timely."

— **BRIDGETT M. DAVIS, author of**
The World according to Fannie Davis

"*We Are Bridges* is a book of history, and as such, it uncovers and recov-
ers the truths no classroom teacher will ever reveal to the children who
need to know them most: 'Let the dead bury the dead, Jesus said, but
here I am: guilty of pining after my dead. Not knowing one's story is
like being buried alive.' More than that, it is a love story, a book of
how—in spite of every obstacle—Black people still make themselves
vulnerable enough to take the leap and fall in (and survive!) love."

— **JERICHO BROWN, author of** *The Tradition*

"Cassandra Lane approaches motherhood, generational trauma, and
hope (and fear) for the future from a multitude of angles in a personal story that is utterly captivating. Her writing is beautiful and truly
embraces readers."

— **JENNIFER BAKER, editor of** *Everyday People*

"*We Are Bridges* is a gorgeous memoir that knits together the past and
present with Cassandra Lane's fierce and beautiful prose. Each sentence pulls readers through the generations, like a song with haunting
lyrics. Lane shows us that family—Black family—is a blazing kaleido-
scope of legacy and memory, reflections illuminated by this talented
writer's acuity and tenderness."

— **DANA JOHNSON, author of** *Elsewhere, California*

"This powerful, beautifully written memoir serves to remind us that our yesterdays need not limit our tomorrows, but that our path forward is forever linked to our history."

— **NORMAN ALADJEM, author of** *From Me to You*

"In *We Are Bridges*, Cassandra Lane boldly investigates the connections between transgenerational trauma, personal love, and the burden of memory. Her heartfelt memoir will stay with you."

— **YZ CHIN, author of** *Though I Get Home*

"*We Are Bridges* considers all that feeds or fails to feed motherhood. Throughout, Lane weaves personal and historical geographies, lineages, upbringings, and upheavals into a complete tapestry validating her glorious existence as a Black mother. Lane's finger, aimed at herself, digs her introspection so deep that what becomes devastated are all the false notions that limit and confound Blackness, growth, parenting. *We Are Bridges* is Lane's lifelong walk with responsibility, with risk—and most of all, with love. It reminds readers that motherhood is never merely witnessing, but a constant testimony of love. And what we beget into this world, what we truly love, is forever linked to a history of liberation."

— **F. DOUGLAS BROWN, author of** *Zero to Three*

"In *We Are Bridges*, Cassandra Lane stretches the boundaries of traditional memoir, incorporating aspects of the unknowable past so as to best illuminate how imagination and speculation color and deepen our truths. This is an important, beautiful work."

— **LOLIS ERIC ELIE, former columnist for the** *Times-Picayune*

"Cassandra Lane has written the book we need now more than ever. Part love story, part historical memoir, *We Are Bridges* explores a legacy of inherited trauma in the context of the author's complicated path toward motherhood. I was engrossed every step of the way."

— **BRENDA MILLER, author of** *An Earlier Life*

"In *We Are Bridges*, Cassandra Lane expertly weaves together personal history, the pain and wonder of inheritance, and a vision of motherhood most infinite. Lane is an honest and unflinching guide, tenderly urging the essential questions: Who are we? Who can we be?"

— **MICHELLE FRANKE, executive director of PEN America Los Angeles**

"Cassandra Lane writes like a dream. *We Are Bridges* is a haunting, absorbing, lyrical, sad, beautiful, and necessary book as we begin to acknowledge the tangible and intangible costs of hundreds of years of slavery."

—DEBRA MONROE, author of *On the Outskirts of Normal*

"In pages both lyrical and evocative, Lane paints a world in which the agonies experienced by earlier generations continue down to the current day; and yet, in the act of creation and empathy, she brings readers and her family into a realm of not quite forgiveness, but reluctant acceptance and awe."

—BERNADETTE MURPHY, author of *Harley and Me*

"Cassandra Lane's *We Are Bridges* is a groundbreaking, lyrical patchwork of historical research, imagined pasts and futures, and personal narrative that tethers together multiple generations of the Bridges family, multiple generations of trauma borne from slavery, and multiple simultaneous truths. *We Are Bridges* is a story that has not yet been told and one that many will feel in their bones."

—KAELYN RICH, author of *Girls Resist!*

"In *We Are Bridges*, Cassandra Lane has written a haunting, lyrical narrative about love, motherhood, and generational trauma, confronting painful truths about her past, her present, and her future. Lane writes with the heart of a poet and the pen of a seasoned journalist as she tells her story with a haunting passion I will never forget. An extraordinary accomplishment."

—ELIZABETH L. SILVER, author of
The Execution of Noa P. Singleton

"Lane weaves a moving and immense narrative of healing intergenerational violence through reportage, witnessing, memory, exhuming the dead, and moving on. Her work illuminates Louise Meriwether's legacy with love and grit. A tour de force filled with the immensity of hope."

—LIS P. SIPIN-GABON, editor and cofounder of
TAYO Literary Magazine

We Are Bridges

A Memoir

Cassandra Lane

THE FEMINIST PRESS
AT THE CITY UNIVERSITY OF NEW YORK
NEW YORK CITY

Published in 2021 by the Feminist Press
at the City University of New York
The Graduate Center
365 Fifth Avenue, Suite 5406
New York, NY 10016

feministpress.org

First Feminist Press edition 2021

 This book is supported in part by an award from the National
Endowment for the Arts.

 This book was made possible thanks to a grant from New York
State Council on the Arts with the support of Governor Andrew
M. Cuomo and the New York State Legislature.

Parts of this book have been previously published in *Everything But the Burden*
(Penguin Random House, 2003); *Daddy, Can I Tell You Something: Black Daughters Speak to Their Fathers* (Sela Press, 2005); and *TheScreamOnline*, and are
reprinted with permission in slightly revised form.

First printing April 2021

Cover illustration by Krystal Quiles
Text design by Frances Ross

Library of Congress Cataloging-in-Publication Data
Names: Lane, Cassandra, 1971- author.
Title: We are bridges : a memoir / Cassandra Lane.
Description: First feminist press edition. | New York, NY : The Feminist
 Press, 2021.
Identifiers: LCCN 2020051097 (print) | LCCN 2020051098 (ebook) | ISBN
 9781952177927 (paperback) | ISBN 9781952177934 (ebook)
Subjects: LCSH: Lane, Cassandra, 1971- | African American mothers--Southern
 States--Biography. | African American families--Southern States. |
 Lynching--Southern States. | Resilience (Personality trait)--Southern
 States.
Classification: LCC E185.86 .L3528 2021 (print) | LCC E185.86 (ebook) |
 DDC 306.85/08996073075--dc23
LC record available at https://lccn.loc.gov/2020051097
LC ebook record available at https://lccn.loc.gov/2020051098

PRINTED IN THE UNITED STATES OF AMERICA

*To my ancestors Burt Bridges and
Mary Magdalene Magee (McGee).*

*And to my mother, Pamela Coar,
for all of your stories and love.*

How can narrative embody life in words and at the same time respect what we cannot know?

—SAIDIYA HARTMAN

Like the phoenix, in you the ancestors come again, rise from the curling red and gray ashes underneath lynching trees. . . . That is what Black reincarnation is. The debt is still owed. We keep making generations to collect our inheritance.

—IMANI PERRY

A PROLOGUE

THIS STORY IS a hybrid—a romance and a horror, a memoir and a fiction—forged out of what is known and what is unknown.

"Sticks and stones may break my bones, but words will never hurt me," we sang as children of the South—as black children of the South. It was a rhyming wall we erected to protect us from harsh words hurled at our bodies, their mission to shoot venom, to curl our brown frames.

The truth is that words, like sticks and stones, like ropes and whips, do injure. As we get older, we press to silence any and all language that elicits pain. But sometimes, buried in this suppressed language is an ancestor—the power in a name.

A different kind of hurt lingers in this stitched void.

I wanted a creation story for my family, although what was lost (stolen) is long covered over by soil I will never be able to locate. When I was young, that was okay with me—the freedom of not being bound to the past, to all that heaviness. But I am a mother now, and freedom means something else to me entirely. I am pregnant with questions, laboring over the unanswered ones tucked in the bosoms of our nation, our ancestors, our living families, and even into my own heart.

Here, I gathered the sticks, picked up the stones, went searching for the rope. Like a bird building her nest, there is filler—string, straw, scraps of paper. Anything to make it hold, make it stick.

MY HISTORY CLASSES in small-town Louisiana schools, and later in a Louisiana college, were led by white teachers whose faces and names have long receded from my memory. They stood, symbols of authority, alongside blackboards against whose surfaces were scribbled small chalked numbers. These dates, chronicling ancient world and US events, slipped and skidded in my memory like shacks in a mudslide. The teachers droned on and on about the dates, their voices cardboard and smoke.

They were hiding something. I didn't know it then. I internalized my thick confusion as a personal intellectual defect. I listened for the stories behind their dates. Something always rang hollow, but you do not know what to ask for when you do not know what is missing.

In study hall, the notes on my index cards mocked me. At test time, my memory failed me. Images of the cards and boards flashed in my mind—blank.

Recoiling from history in the same manner that I recoiled from calculus, my defense mechanism became, as I grew older, a proud declaration that I wore like a badge: I'm right-brained. I love words and art and nature, sensual and imaginative things.

I didn't realize that history too—even when presented with a capital H—can be subjective, can be a work of the imagination. Or omission. When I was growing up, the old folks used to say, not telling the whole truth is a lie.

The word *history* hails from the Greek *historia*, which means knowing, learned, to see, to know. One definition states, "An account of what has or might have happened, especially in the form of a narrative, play, story, or tale."

Might have happened.

It can also mean "something that belongs to the past" or "someone or something regarded as no longer important, relevant, useful."

To "make history" is to "be or do something important enough to be recorded."

As a student, I didn't learn the histories of my people or my people's people. There must have been sections, or subsections, about Africa and slavery and Jim Crow and the civil rights movement. Right? But when I try to recall my education, which spanned the late seventies to the early nineties, it is a fog to which I cannot connect.

Curiously, I chose to study journalism in undergrad, becoming the editor of my campus newspaper and then, fresh out of college, a newspaper reporter.

"How are *you* going to be a journalist?" my mother had asked worriedly when I first declared my major. "You don't . . . *talk* to people."

It was true: While she is all water and electricity and spoken words, I was timid and awkward and nervous. Petrified wood. Somewhat mum. A universe of words swirled inside me, trapped.

But the listening skills I had honed as a girl, eavesdropping on the conversations of my adult relatives and hanging around my grandparents and their friends, got me through as a young reporter. I learned what kinds of questions to ask. My eyes were big and unguarded, two pools reflecting what people read as compassion and interest. They spilled their responses into my ears. I carried reporter's notebooks and pens and mini tape recorders as if they were missing limbs I had rescued. I pored over my chicken-scratch notes and transcribed recordings, piecing together my sources' stories. The recorded interviews were always superior to my shorthand. When I used a recorder, I was not distracted by trying to write down my subjects' words.

I could zero in on what they were saying, I could look them in their eyes. The recorded interviews captured their vocal tics, their sighs, their pauses, their tears and laughter, their "no, no—don't put that part in."

I was an antenna out in the world, tuning into stranger after stranger: astronauts and cancer survivors, city officials and celebrities. Somewhere along the way, I began to think, and then write, about my own family of origin.

How do we connect to all these floating lines of reportage and history and dates? In newspaper columns, I introduced some of the characters of my own life, especially holding reverence for my maternal grandparents, who had died by the mid-1990s.

Their voices had never been recorded, and this void haunts me still. They had been disenfranchised all their days on earth and now disembodied with no audio record of their embodiment. In my hours of greatest need, I strain to remember my grandparents' cadences and vernacular, their singing and hums and deep-throated chants.

IN 2017 I sat on the other side of the recording box. The *New York Times* had put out a call for essays about becoming a mother. I wrote a short essay about my conflicted relationship with motherhood and sent it in.

I wrote about how, at sixteen, I had decided, fervently, that I would not become a mother. Never, ever that.

I'd seen motherhood, black motherhood, up close: Mama working long hours and raising us children without our fathers' assistance. My grandmother cooking and cleaning from sun up to sun down after we moved in with her and my grandfather; this when she was in her seventies and eighties and had long ago raised her eight children and should have been enjoying her freedom. And there was my great-grandmother, Mary, who had only had one child, my grandfather, but that birth story was tragic. My great-grandfather, Burt Bridges, was lynched before Mary could deliver their baby for him to hold and to cherish.

No, motherhood would not dot my path. I would not bring another black child into a world of such oppression and lack. But I started having sex at sixteen and got pregnant at seventeen, the age my mother was when she had me. I had an abortion as quickly as I could. My pledge not to give birth lasted for nearly twenty years, until something within me started shifting, and I yearned (predictably, perhaps) for a child.

At thirty-six, after a determined ride in the other direction, my life changed drastically: I became a mother.

My story was selected as part of the *New York Times*'s series Conception: Six Stories of Becoming a Mother. To bring our stories to life in a new way, the producer, a visual journalist, would fly to each of our cities to have us retell our stories in sound studios. She would then edit those stories and hire animators to create moving animations to our recorded voices. The result would be a collection of animated videos that the paper would publish online.

The producer found a studio that was five minutes from my job at Dodger Stadium in Los Angeles, where I was working at the time. We made plans to meet there one evening after work.

I was nervous. I had agreed to speak aloud an intimate personal story—a story that even most of my family didn't know— to an international audience. I worried, too, how lingering bronchitis symptoms, including a raspy voice and deep chest cough that sometimes felt as though it were strangling me, would impact the recording.

"Don't worry about the cough," the producer said. "We can edit that out."

It was early May. Jacaranda trees flowered the Los Angeles streets with their falling purple blossoms. The studio was Echo

Park cool. With forty thousand square feet of "sound sanctuary," its interior was draped in a moody, retro style: jewel-colored walls, wall textiles, throw pillows, and rugs in earthy boho prints. My producer was a white woman, probably ten or fifteen years my junior. I handed her a bag of Dodgers hats and T-shirts, and she gushed. She introduced me to our sound engineer, who gave me a laid-back, friendly smile.

A couple of guitars sat in stands on the floor, and I thought of my mother, a gospel guitarist. The producer motioned for me to sit behind a mic stand that was lowered in front of a wide, burnt-orange leather armchair. I sat down. The arms, gargantuan, were too high for me to rest on comfortably, but I tried to relax.

There was no warming up; the producer jumped right in.

"Let's start from the beginning. Tell me about your childhood."

I stuttered. The poetic river I'd been able to create in my essay was all of a sudden dried up; my words jumbled and meandered as I talked about my childhood, my mother's divorce, our move back into her parents' house, and how my great-grandmother was also living there.

Trying to tie it all to the motherhood connection, I brought up Grandma Mary's lynching story. "She was pregnant with my grandfather when the father of her child, my great-grandfather, was lynched in Mississippi in 1904," I said.

The producer paused and raised one eyebrow slightly. Then she tilted her head.

"1904," she said. "That was a long time ago."

The year sounded so ancient coming from her mouth. It sounded like something that "belongs to the past . . . regarded as no longer important, relevant, useful."

I felt silly, scolded, and silenced all at once. It was, again, 2017. I was forty-six and raising a ten-year-old son in the middle of one of the most diverse cities in the world. I had left the South behind sixteen years earlier. Why couldn't I let the heaviness of my family's past go?

Shame and anger whirled inside me, although I couldn't quite put my finger on what piece of her response I had interpreted as injury, whether she meant it to be or not. Was it the subtle move of her head or brow, a shift in her tone, or the use of the phrase "a long time ago"?

As the interview continued, I sat there telling her the parts she wanted to hear, stopping to hack loudly when I could no longer suppress my coughs. I gulped water and wished that I had also swallowed the year of Burt's lynching, that I had ended with "my great-grandfather was lynched."

Period.

But 1904 is one of the historical years I know; it is seared into my cells and memory and writings about my family. As a fellow storyteller, I had wanted the producer to explore with me how the lynching story of my history—a man torn from his unborn child through one of the worst forms of racial violence this country has witnessed—might be a part of my psyche and my conception story.

It—1904—was a long time ago, yes. Still, those long-time-ago people were my grandparents and my great-grandparents, and for that alone, I love them. Burt was lynched nearly seventy years before my birth, but Mary survived, and I remember her. I remember bits and pieces of her. I remember the bitter and sweet of her. And since she lived until her nineties, Burt might have lived until his nineties too. His living might have spelled a better life for his son and his son's children, for me and my child.

My lynching quote didn't make it into the producer's final cut. I understand. I was sharing a piece of my story, but she had the right to edit her final product as she saw fit.

Besides, I, too, was a revisionist. I told her my abortion story, how I married a man who was likewise staunchly opposed to having children, but I did not divulge how I destroyed that marriage with an affair. I said, instead, that we went our separate ways, implying that it was based on my changing views about parenthood. When the story aired, I emailed my ex-husband. "It's just a slice of my larger story," I wrote. "I will tell my whole story about what happened later."

He said he understood.

My elders' words sounded in my ears: *not telling the whole truth is a lie.*

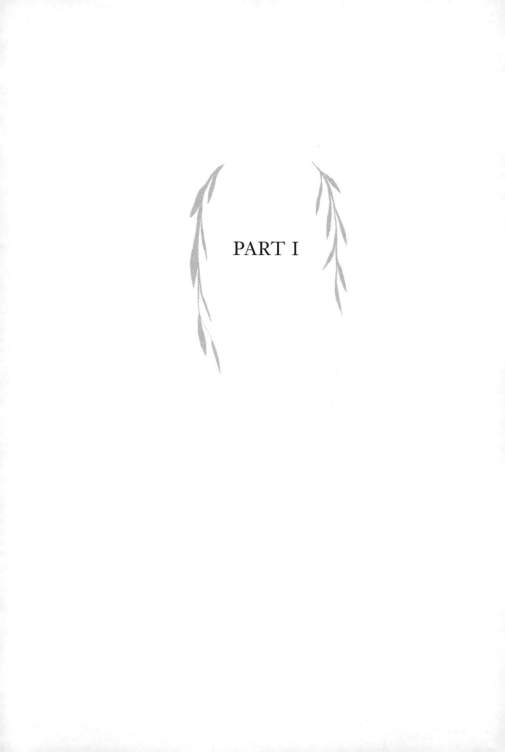

PART I

IN THE ABSENCE OF BLOOD

IN THE FALL of 2006, I sat on the bathroom floor of a new house I had just rented with a man I barely knew, our backs held up by the wall. I lifted a pregnancy test up to the light. We gazed at it, the odd plastic wand revealing that something, another human being, was growing inside me. Marcus and I looked into each other's eyes. His pupils mirrored mine, swooning with disbelief and . . . something else.

"What do you want to do?" we asked each other simultaneously.

"I don't know," I said, "but I don't *not* want to keep it." I clenched my teeth in a painful grin, my eyebrows two question marks as I searched his face, his body language, his Adam's apple.

"Me either." A sharp piece of laughter shot past the shock in his throat. "Me either. I don't not want to keep it either."

"Oh my God. Oh my God. Does this mean that I—that we—are going to have a baby?"

We had met that January, the weekend after New Year's, at a hip lounge in LA's Silver Lake neighborhood. We moved in together by that summer and were now staring at a positive pregnancy test only nine months after learning each other's names. No, we didn't know each other at all, but you couldn't have told us that at the time. We talked for hours on the phone and in person. We made love nearly as much. We shared our life stories with each other—long talks into the night are the stuff of early romance. Those early days, weeks, and months of a relationship are always colored by lust and feelings of love. The hard and mundane stuff remained veiled and muffled in the sweet orbs of infatuation.

I had, for example, no real understanding of what it meant to be in a relationship with a man who had adolescent boys and what it would mean to introduce a new child into that mix. Marcus's sons, Immanuel, who was fourteen, and Yanni, who was eleven, were with their mother the weekend I took the pregnancy test. How would we tell them the news? They had not warmed up to me in the way I had hoped. Mostly, they stayed to themselves, quiet and withdrawn. We had moved too quickly for them, had pulled them headfirst into the whirlwind of our connection. And since Marcus had agreed to keep the boys full-time while his ex-wife got on her feet, our moving in together had meant uprooting the boys' lives from a one-bedroom apartment with their father into a three-bedroom that I had picked out.

I was certain they would grow ecstatic when they saw the place. But having their own rooms in a clean and beautiful space full of light was nothing if their own mother wasn't in it. I didn't get that then. I took their sullenness and rejections personally.

"What will the boys think?" I asked Marcus.

He smiled. "You worry too much. They'll be fine."

"Really, though. What are we gonna do?" My question was a raised whisper.

"Let's sleep on it," Marcus said. "Let me know how you feel in the morning." He said it like it was the most rational thing to do. He was grinning, and I was grinning too. We scooted closer together and wrapped our arms around each other, our butts numb against the tile floor.

I was seventeen the first time I conceived. It was September

1988. I got pregnant in my mother's hometown of DeRidder, Louisiana, and ended that life while it was still nascent, soft, alien, and invisible to me, in my father's hometown of Beaumont, Texas. After the abortion, I suppressed the experience to the recesses of my marrow. Other than my boyfriend, no one else knew about that pregnancy, and for a long time after, whenever I filled out medical forms, I denied that I had ever been pregnant. No, I had not been a black pregnant teen, I lied defiantly, writing in a zero each time a form asked for the number of times I had been pregnant. I detested stereotypes, refused to admit falling prey to them.

My mother had been a single black woman raising children in our small town of watchful eyes and gossiping tongues, moving in with her parents after her divorce from my father, with whom she had two children, my sister Dena and me. Over the next twelve years, she had three more children with men who were not interested in being fathers. Mama worked a government job that paid her a salary that felt like punishment. She fought off bitterness with each promotion she deserved but did not receive and pushed herself to try harder for the next one.

In the same way, after long bouts of romantic disillusionment, she would give love a try again. She was pregnant with my youngest sibling, her fifth child, when I became pregnant: mother and daughter, pregnant at the same time. I stood holding my newborn baby brother, Dane, in my arms in the hospital room just a few months after I had aborted the fetus I was carrying. I refused to add to my mother's burden, to her shame, and to her financial woes. And there had been no point in telling her; she was staunch in her antiabortion stance. And so I, her quietly obstinate firstborn, held her just-out-of-the-womb lastborn mere weeks after I had aborted what would have been her firstborn grandchild. I stood in the middle of her hospital room, transfixed to a spot several feet from her bed. Light streamed in from the windows. I inhaled the scent of new human flesh, savoring what my mother had provided from her body and what I had deleted from mine. I had come within months of repeating my mother's pattern: becoming a first-time mother at seventeen. Even though I dreamed of marrying my boyfriend one day, in my view, young marriage and young motherhood were both tragic things. I wanted to live—to study and travel abroad and throw elaborate parties I used to act out while washing dishes, pretending the silverware were the bodies of glamorous people and the dishwater was the pool in which they swam and lounged. I wanted *real* romance, the kind I had learned about when I was in junior high school and read my mother's Harlequin and Silhouette novels on the sly—holding the slim and steamy volumes between shaky fingers while I crouched in a closet. I was a witness to my mother's failed romances, her pregnancies, and the hardships of child-rearing. I wanted to be free of all the chains and stains of motherhood.

A LATE BLOOMER in all things, I didn't start menstruating until age sixteen. The blood had arrived, finally, while I was sitting on my grandmother's braided rug in her den one afternoon, the same den where my mother had married my father when she was also just sixteen—a marriage everyone knew was doomed to fail. My period had come with a force, bringing with it deep, heavy aches in my pelvis. I was sitting in French class when it returned, but without the usual preliminary pains, after my abortion. I had on a peach-and-white striped mock turtle-neck and narrow A-line peach skirt—an outfit I had proudly purchased with my own money from my job as a checkout clerk at Piggly Wiggly.

I had traveled across the Louisiana-Texas state lines just a few days earlier to lie on an examination table and have a doctor suck the embryo out of my uterus. Back at school, I tried to be my normal self again, giggling, keeping my lips glossed, gossiping with friends, but I suspected that I was forever changed. That day in French class, I felt liquid stick against the crotch of my panties. I pressed my thighs together, panicking. When the bell rang, I remained seated.

My best friends, Loretta and two girls named Melanie, were also in the class.

"Girl, let's go," Melanie V. said as students rustled about, and I still hadn't packed up my things.

"I can't stand up," I said.

"What? Why?"

"I think my skirt is messed up."

Melanie S.'s eyes widened. She took off her jacket. "Here. Wrap this around yourself."

The girls formed a partial fence around me as I tied the sleeves around my waist. I stood up without looking back at the seat.

"You've got to go home," they said, pushing me toward the office. I was ashamed. How had I gotten to be this old and messed myself at school? The doctor had not talked to me about my period, about my body, and I had mistakenly thought that my period would come the following month according to my usual menstruation calendar.

I stood in the office, waiting for Uncle Cricket to pick me up since my mother was working twenty miles out of town on the army base and my grandparents no longer drove. My AP English literature teacher waltzed into the office, her head high, her narrow nose riding the air like an aristocrat. My breath caught. I was both awed by and afraid of her. She stopped and looked down at me.

"Miss Lane, what is going on?" she asked, except it did not feel like a question.

"I—I'm sick," I said. "I have to go home."

She looked at the jacket around my waist. "I see."

She walked away curtly. I had the sinking feeling that I had let everyone down and that they knew it without knowing it, like the blood that had been there and then disappeared and then returned, concealed only by thin layers of clothing.

I COULD NOT sleep the night Marcus and I read the results of my pregnancy test. I ran calculations in my head. It was late October, which meant I had conceived, once again, in September.

By my calculations, my baby would be born just before summer, a month or so after my thirty-sixth birthday. Marcus would turn forty-one that July. Were we too old? And could we even afford to bring a baby into the world on my new teacher salary and his income as a Hollywood tour-bus driver and budding real estate agent? In just a few years, his boys would be leaving the nest. Having another baby would mean starting over for him.

To have a baby together, born of his blood and mine, would be a mutual agreement to do everything within our power to give our child stability, love, and room to expand. It would mean modeling a healthy love of self and each other. My role as mother to this baby would be different from what it was with Marcus's sons, whom I told to view me as a kind of mentor and insisted that they would never have to feel forced to call me Mom should their father and I marry. I was there but largely hands-off, leaving heavy decisions to Marcus. After all, I was essentially still a stranger. Deep down, I knew that despite our embryonic love for each other, despite an attraction that could, with our track record, wane as powerfully as it came, we should not be bringing new life into the middle of our already complicated web of family histories and personal character flaws. Even so, I hoped to give our child a chance to thrive.

When I met Marcus, my first marriage had been over for

less than a year, and I was trying to extricate myself from—while still holding on to—the affair that had destroyed that marriage. The affair, unsurprisingly, had turned sour, and meeting Marcus just after New Year's 2006 had felt like a breath of fresh air. He, too, was in the midst of trying to piece his life back together after his marital breakup—taking classes in real estate in between his other jobs. I don't believe he harbored any desires of parenting another child.

But we were careless and foolish, and full of desire. Two broken romantics clinging to each other and nothing at all. Whether it had been the turning of that mythical biological clock or a root-level change of my mind to remain childless, I felt my heart racing with excitement over the knowledge of life growing inside me. Being in massive Los Angeles with no family around; trying to make a go of it with my career, new love, and art; and now a baby on the way—the very idea was ludicrous.

Which made me want it even more. I could feel contradictory squeals scurrying up my throat.

I was once again without blood, and this absence made me remember an old saying my mother liked to repeat: *blood is always thicker than water*. Family should come first, always, is what she meant. I have been that wayward daughter, moving far away from family, treating friends more like blood.

The morning after the test, Marcus and I made love. Yes, I want you. Yes, I want this. Yes, I want this baby. It was a Saturday, one day before he would pick up his sons from their mother's place. I was grateful to have a few hours alone with him as we made a decision about the latest shift in our lives. After showering, I gazed at my body, at my stomach, in the floor-length mirror, trying to imagine it stretched and swollen.

I searched online for "best ob-gyns in Los Angeles." Reviewers gushed over a doctor whose practice was just fifteen minutes away. After the doctor confirmed my pregnancy a few days later, I called my mother and sisters on three-way. We spanned three geographies; I was the only one on the West Coast. Mama, my middle sister Dena, and my brothers all lived in Orlando, and my youngest sister, Michie, lived in Virginia with her husband. My mother's sole grandchild was Dena's son, Andre, who was thirteen.

I stood in the bonus room that sat at the rear of my bedroom. It was surrounded by windows. Sunny and cheery, it would be the perfect baby's room.

"I have something to tell you, ladies," I said into the phone sheepishly.

"Oh Lord," Dena said. "What's going on? Is everything okay?"

"Yeah, yeah. Everything's okay. It's just that . . . it's just that . . . I'm pregnant!"

The phones erupted in an avalanche of squeals and screams and laughter. "Whaaaaaat?!" The long screech came from all three of the women.

"Sand!" Mama finally said, catching her breath. "Baby, I am so happy for you and so proud of you." There was joy in her voice but also concern. "How does Marcus feel about this? Oh my goodness, we haven't even met him yet."

"He's good, he's good," I said. "He's happy." I could have called them while he was still at home but had wanted a private moment with my family, especially since they had not met him—and because I knew my announcement would rock their minds.

"This is great, but I thought you didn't want kids," Michie said. "How do you feel?"

I snort-laughed. "I didn't," I said. "I used to not, anyway. I feel oddly fine. I'm still in shock too though."

"A new baby in the family," Dena said. "About time. Maybe you'll move back home finally."

The tinge of resentment in my sister's voice was clear. I had chosen to move so far away perhaps to be free from the expectations she found herself under now that she and Mama lived in the same town again.

"Well," I said, "Florida has never been my home."

"Well," she said, mockingly, "home is where family is."

Next I told my friend April, who was also in her late thirties and child-free. She grew quiet on the phone, but it took me a while to catch on.

"What's wrong?" I asked, halting my excitement.

She wondered how I had allowed myself to "fall into" motherhood after swearing it off for most of my adult life. She feared that it would spell the end of me. She feared that I would lose myself in the man and the baby—that we had moved too fast.

"It's a cliché for women of a certain age to want children," she said. "You never wanted kids before. Why now? I think women start to feel the societal pressure they've kept at bay for years, and they start to wonder if they've made a mistake; they can almost feel their eggs shriveling, and they panic. It's such a trap. This world is overpopulated as it is. We really don't need any more children in it just for more pain and suffering. And that man just wants you to help him take care of the kids he already has."

"No, they have a mother," I said. "I don't want or care to take her place."

I understood what she was saying, though, and in many ways I agreed. Perhaps I was a walking cliché.

But I felt like a miracle. And this "miracle" pregnancy felt larger than I was. It felt like a path for me to follow through to the end this time.

HANGED INHERITANCES

I WAS IN my freshman year of college when I heard, for the first time, a recording of Billie Holiday singing "Strange Fruit." I repeatedly listened to her sing both "Don't Explain" and "Strange Fruit"—the former about a wayward lover, and the latter about the black victims of a murderous South. The images and moods in these two songs, the hushing and howling, Billie's voice ringing with a huskiness my fingers could almost touch—all of it would merge in my mind until I saw lipstick smeared over twisted mouths and dead eyes bulging with hopes of greener pastures. I listened, again and again, until lovers' bodies and bloody roots entwined, and a sweet rot emanated from my own mouth.

It seemed as though Billie were singing directly to our family. It seemed as though she were seeing us—the whole line of us, at least as far back as the age of Jim Crow.

Psychologists call it "trauma ghosting"—the body's ability to "remember" a trauma that happened earlier in life or in an ancestor's life. It can manifest as an extreme and inappropriate reaction to anything that "reminds" the body of that early trauma. I think about my aversion to the stage, how my body shakes from its innermost core at the prospect of a crowd in front of me. Perhaps my body sees an audience, senses it, and remembers a mob staring at my great-grandfather Burt as he is about to be lynched, or as another ancestor is being whipped in front of a crowd, or as another is standing on top of a platform being sold.

Let the dead bury the dead, Jesus said, but here I am: guilty of pining after my dead. Not knowing one's story is like being buried alive. The living pretend they don't know you're under the soil, but there you are, plain as dirt, providing a foundation over which they trample and build and move on with their lives.

A FEW WEEKS into my pregnancy, I dashed into my go-to import store, an open warehouse of a place filled with home interior fashions and art we so loosely exoticize, materials we cloak and surround ourselves with to feel worldly and cultured. It is a chain version of an export store, bringing "the world" to those of us who can't regularly afford to travel to faraway places or frequent exclusive import/export boutiques. I was stopping by the store to pick up some small percussion instruments for a volunteer workshop I was teaching at an elementary school.

Inspired by Afro-Caribbean music, I named the workshop Drumming Up Words and intended to marry song, syllable counting, storytelling, and poetry with the beating and shaking of percussion instruments. To add to the collection of instruments that I was bringing from home—djembe drums, a wooden xylophone, rain sticks, a triangle, bells—I wanted to see if the store had a few small last-minute items, such as a tambourine or maracas.

In the small toy section, I spotted some tiny plastic-rimmed tambourines. Determined to find something better, I bent down and combed my eyes over the bottom shelf. Something jumped out at me: bright colors on shiny metallic. I picked up the toy and my heart skipped. My hand flew to my mouth. The word *hangman* was blazoned across the toy's packaging.

I raised it closer to my face. No, my eyes were not playing tricks on me. The metal box contained a magnetic version of the game that so many of us played in grade school. Except the letters were painted on magnetic pieces waiting to be spelled correctly or else the child (five and older) would be hanged. Unlike the stick bodies of our long-ago drawings, the "man" in this game was a realistic depiction of a human: a half-smiling white cowboy, chin full of stubble, a wide hat on his head, a rope around his neck, and an incomplete body. The rest of his body parts were just waiting to meet him, courtesy of the loser.

"This is not okay," I said aloud, straining to get up. "This is not okay." I wanted to buy the game as proof but didn't want to be caught buying it. A few people, at ease on that quiet afternoon, passed by me and glanced at my stricken face as I stood in the middle of the toy section with my mouth agape.

I pulled out my cell and took a picture of the hangman game.

I was grateful that I was not yet a mother. What if I had been with my child, innocently looking for toys, when we discovered the hangman game? What if my child begged and begged me for it, and I, still in shock, had to explain why we could never buy such a game? At least now I knew to watch out for it. At least now I knew that I could be in the middle of Los Angeles shopping at a store that promotes a "global" take on living and run smack dab into a reminder of lynchings, wrapped in shiny, cartoonish packaging.

At home, I opened my computer and searched for the hangman game on Amazon, and there it was, bright as day. Parents love it, starred reviews revealed. And the product description made no bones about the objective and consequences of the game: "Guess an incorrect letter, and a body part is added. Solve the word before you get hung!"

A take 'n' play anywhere game. All for the price of $9.99.

A MEMORY (what feels like a memory) comes to me:

A white boy is writing his name—*Lloyd*—and mine on a blackboard, drawing a line between us. The chalk squeaks and

strains against the board as the boy creates another long verti-
cal line—his hangman's pole—and a series of short blank lines
beneath it. He turns to me with a sneer and the most difficult
phrase he can fathom locked in his head, which is covered with
silvery blond hair and filled with tricks.

We are in second grade, and every year, we stand next to
each other when it's time to line up in alphabetical order. A veil
of camaraderie has emerged from this mash-up, but we are not
really friends.

I sit in the middle row surrounded by vacant desks, praying
that my brain will fill in all the blanks of Lloyd's person, place,
or thing.

I glance out the window where the rest of our classmates are
running and squealing with delight, their faces glowing with
sweat. Why have I chosen to spend my recess in a cold, quiet
classroom filled with the grin stretching across Lloyd's face and
the anxiety over losing pinching at my chest?

"R!"

I call out the letter first because it seems to be a staple ingredient of most words, but there is no r, and there is not even a t—
none of the usual standbys apply. Letter by letter, the boy hangs
my errors, drawing in the body parts of the little stick person:
head first, then neck, then right arm. If this boy were just a
teeny bit nice, he'd give me facial features and fingers; he'd bless
me with a triangle skirt, endowing me with more time.

I am stuck. I run out of the safe consonants and vowels. I
feel caged and can sense my stomach sinking. Half of my stick
body dangles on the edge of the pole as my opponent greedily
waits to shout out my defeat.

I sit frozen in my bone-hard seat, feeling myself diminish-
ing, centimeter by centimeter. The line extending from the
expressionless, carved-out head on the blackboard is a vein in
my neck.

But how was I losing? How was I losing to this boy—a C student?

I was the spelling bee champion. Our teacher, Mrs. Crain, had called me "smart," and her praise had been like gold.

"Where's Miss Spelling Bee now?" Lloyd teases as, time after time, he fills my stick body in on the chalked gurney.

"Hung!" he rings. I picture a little silver bell dangling at the back of his throat.

Hung!

The word echoes through the room. Fear and saliva rise in my throat.

The school bell rings. The other kids trickle back into the classroom, moist and happy. Lloyd does not offer the answer to his puzzle, and I do not ask.

Better to not know what hanged me.

THESE GHOSTS OF memories are scattered across the landscape of my childhood recollections, much of them inseparable from my imagination and interpretations. Unbeknownst to Lloyd and me, we were players in a game much bigger than us. Unlike our parents, our only school option was the integrated school. Our teacher was black. My mother's high school had not integrated until the year after she left, in 1970.

I do not know if Lloyd's parents had taught him about segregation, but already I knew my place. I was fighting against this unspoken yet pervasive contract. I was fighting, as stealthily and stubbornly as it was. Through the sheer power of my supposed brilliance in those early grade-school years, I was attempting to break out of the mold that had been set for me. I was smart, they said, my family and Mrs. Crain, but they were all black, and Lloyd had proven them wrong. If I couldn't hold my brain up as a prize to say, *Look, I am more than you say*, what good was I?

Marcus and I spoke often about our childhood moments of feeling devalued, and we swore to shower our child with love and affirmations, impenetrable shields from the mental arrows that would one day come, long before we had to fear the path of bullets.

This muscle of building up a child was already formed in Marcus. I had witnessed him pumping up his older sons and trying to infuse them with the power of who they could be, even when they were slipping and drawn to the streets that had once swallowed him. Marcus had not had a father to guide him, so he was teaching himself how to gift fatherhood to his flesh and blood.

I was rushing against time to locate and pick up all my missing parts, the fragments of which I had not felt the need to really salvage because I had not had the responsibility of young black life under my hands.

I was woefully unprepared.

"I-PP-I-SS-I-SS-I-M!" We would sing-spell the state backward as children. Backward Mississippi. I didn't know yet that Mississippi was one of my motherlands. I didn't know yet that someone in our bloodline had been lynched in one of its backwoods. But I believe my body knew.

However, even more than early sensations and explorations, my pregnancy boomeranged me back to my family and our past. The idea of carrying a child to full term, of trying to see with my mind's eye each group of embryonic cells forming beneath my own, ignited awe and joy within me at the same time that it reignited an old preoccupation: Who were our people? Who were we before Grandma Mary settled in Louisiana? I needed to know—for my child. I had been in Los Angeles for five years, but for the first time, the physical distance from my family mattered. Where the two thousand miles separating us had once felt like freedom, now with new family blood forming inside me, I felt untethered and worlds away from my family and our ancestral home in Louisiana; from my now-dead grandparents, my mother's parents, Grandmama Avis and Papa Houston; and from Houston's mother, Grandma Mary, the relative who, in many ways, represents the origin of our family history, our oldest, most visceral connection to the past, since most things—other relatives' names, our ancestry, gravesites—are unknown.

My scant genealogical knowledge stretched back only three generations, past my own parents and grandparents, landing squarely in the grotesque history of my great-grandparents, Mary Magdalene Magee (or McGee—I have seen both spellings in family Bibles), and her one true love: Burt Bridges, the father of her only child, Houston, who birthed a mini nation. Burt and Mary's story is a tale of young love, gestation, and lynching. While Mary was likely still pregnant with Houston, Burt had been lynched in Mississippi in 1904. Many in our family did not know about this legacy. I did not want my child to be likewise blind to it—and to its lasting impacts.

By the time I left for college, and before I first listened to Billie Holiday, I had finally learned some fragments of our family's history thanks to the storytelling tongues of my mother and Uncle Cricket. They told me what they knew. Through them, I collected the little broken-off bones of our American lynching story, and day after day while I was pregnant, I entered my writing room—the bonus space that would later house the baby's bed in addition to my desk—to conjure up some semblance of that story—the story of Burt Bridges.

Burt Bridges.

The name Burt derives from an Old English word that meant "bright" and a German one translating to "that which is due or proper." It was a nickname for someone who had fulfilled his obligations properly.

Burt Bridges.

The man whose lineage they tried to destroy.

I said his name and wrote it into existence. As far as I knew, there was no gravestone carved with his name, no material proof. There were no birth or death certificates. There was no record of his and Mary's love, no photograph, no yellowed note.

Using Papa Houston's delayed birth certificate as evidence, Uncle Cricket told me that the lynching likely took place in or around Holmesville in Pike County, Mississippi. Looking at a map of the South, you can see how the top line of Louisiana's boot holds up the bowels of southern Mississippi from Wilkinson to parts of Marion County. Pike County is right in the middle of that. Both born sometime in the 1880s, Burt and Mary had come of age shortly after the fall of the Reconstruction era, when white people were viciously looking to squash the spirit, and very humanity, of any black person who might have been inspired by that brief period of progress. They swung rope after lynching rope. They burned "black wall streets."

Other than Grandma Mary's caged memories, and Papa Houston's birth certificate, we have no recollections or records of our family's story during that time; we have not been able to uncover any facts to back up Mary and Burt's splintered narrative. Burt was just one of the thousands of black people lynched in some town, some backwoods, or some city in these United States. Was there even a newspaper blurb written about his death? I have searched old newspaper accounts in books and online that mention some "unknown Negro lynched" (as though the victim was unknown to his family and his community) and wondered if the nameless man was Burt.

THE HOUSE ON ELM STREET

FOR PARTS OF the 1970s and 1980s, four generations of our family lived under the roof at 202 Elm Street in DeRidder, Louisiana: Papa Houston and Grandmama Avis, who bought the house in 1943 and raised the last of their eight children in it; Grandma Mary, in her nineties, twice widowed and no longer able to look after her own home and farm; my mother, who left my abusive father to return to the home in which she was born; and us, her children.

When Grandma Mary wasn't making tea cakes or sitting out on the front porch, she sat like an ancient relic in the back bedroom. I have only one picture of her: a digital copy of an old photograph that my sister found inside one of Mama's photo boxes. The image is slightly fuzzy, but her face is brazen and alive as she looks dead at the camera. Her head is held high; her gray hair, parted on the left side, frames her olive-black face; her mouth is in a straight line; her eyebrows are stretched high above her eyes as though she is questioning the photographer's choice to photograph her. Rather than forbidding the act, her expression seems to ask, *Are you sure you want to capture this?* I squint to find myself, or anyone in our family, in her features. I look for the young Mary she once was, trying to imagine her full of hopes and dreams and then trauma and grief.

In the image, Grandma Mary is sitting in her shiny,

tobacco-colored leatherlike recliner, her left elbow propped on the arm of the chair. She is draped in a white housecoat of washed-out red roses. Her forearms, especially the right one, are swollen with pus and blood, and I can remember my little-girl fingers sinking into her gelatinous flesh to wake her after she had fallen asleep sitting up. Her fingers are gnarled with arthritis, her knuckles knotted and determined as she holds on to the edges of a perfect brown square that could be an oversize book or a folded piece of cloth.

I once spoke to my mother about the photograph. She was the one aiming the lens at Grandma Mary that day. She had bought a Ricoh camera on layaway from Fingerhut and became obsessed with documenting family life. The brown square Grandma Mary was holding in the photograph was not a book. It was a piece of perfectly cut cardboard that she used to fan herself with and swat at mosquitoes and flies.

And ghosts.

I wish I had known to talk to Grandma Mary about her past, but I doubt she would have blessed my quest. She would have swatted me away as well. When it came to releasing the story of Burt, she was no willing griot. Her preference was to keep the past in the past, but with a new generation growing inside me, I felt my blood quickening. I was thirsty for knowledge. Soon I would feel my baby stirring around inside me, a ticking time bomb of new life embedded with our DNA—a connection that called me back to my ancestors whether they wanted me or not.

After Burt was lynched, Mary married a distant cousin, John Buckley, a farmer, a man she did not love but whom her elders urged her to marry because she was a new mother.

Mary and her new family migrated to Louisiana. The move was a life-saving one, according to Uncle Cricket. John had gotten into a scuffle with a white man—perhaps the sharecropper of the farm he worked on—and killed him. He and Mary fled under the cover of night. In Louisiana, they reinvented themselves and witnessed the birth of new generations.

Grandma Mary only gave into family members' questions about Burt a few times over the ensuing decades, and only after much badgering. I suppose her silences were meant to protect the family from the horror of his death. She had moved on so that Burt's descendants could have a clean slate and not be bogged down in hatred and resentment. Her silence must have protected her, too, from such burdens. But in moving on and sealing history, she also deprived us of Burt's beauty. What did his laughter sound like? Was it a sudden bellow like mine or a series of swallowed chuckles like Uncle James's?

What Mary eventually released were crumbs that opened up our hunger, droplets that let us know we were thirsty.

She gave us two morsels of bread.

When my mother was a girl, pressing her grandmother to tell her something, anything, about her father's biological father, Grandma Mary would become vexed—but once, after my mother grew to be a young woman, a smile kissed Grandma Mary's lips, and she looked at her granddaughter with girlish, secretive eyes: "He was some good looking, I tell you. He was one fine man."

Then her eyes and mood darkened. Her lips turned down like milk turned sour—curdled.

"Them white folk hated my Burt," she continued. "They called him a uppity nigger, and they hanged him."

The last time she said his name was just before she died in the fall of 1982.

"She was lying there on the nursing home bed, and she burst into tears," my mother recalled. "It was just before she became really ill. She said, 'Them white folk was scared of my Burt, baby. One morning we found my Burt hanging!'

"And then, you know what she told me? She said, 'Baby, I'm

not gonna talk about my Burt no more.' She was still crying. After all those years."

I lapped up Mama's story like a fresh calf at her mother's teat.

WHENEVER THE SCREEN DOOR squawks open at the house across the street from mine, it reminds me of the house I grew up in.

Sound is like that. The heart is like that.

Our front screen door would screech open with a long, noisy yawn each time someone came in or went out of the house. That door was full of stories—decades of stories. It was a revolving door—never locked during daylight or evening hours—a passageway for our ventures into and back out of the world, a clearing in the woods for extended family, neighbors, and other townsfolk looking for some of what Mary and Avis had to offer: a cup of brown sugar, cornmeal, or flour; a listening ear, a prayer.

DeRidder was an old Kansas City railroad town that a Dutch railroad financier named after his sister-in-law, Ella de Ridder. White men who "discover" places get to name, or rename, them after whomever or whatever they please. The Dutchman's treasure was incorporated as a town in 1903, and its town motto, "We Dwell in Possibilities," is taken from Emily Dickinson's poem, "I Dwell in Possibilities."

Burt was lynched around the same time that DeRidder became a town. After the lynching, Mary and her new husband, John—Mississippi escapees, sharecroppers—moved through central Louisiana until settling on their own land and in their own home in the Old Heights section of DeRidder.

Was DeRidder poetry for Mary? Was it a possibility?

It was somewhat of a cocoon, as it proved safer than the lynching spirit of Mississippi, a place to which Mary never returned. Yet DeRidder dwells as the seat of a parish named after a Confederate general: P. G. T. Beauregard. Beauregard's legacy includes the story of his change of heart toward the black people he had fought to keep in slavery forever. After his side lost the war, he retreated to New Orleans with a hanging head, and somewhere in that state of humility, he began to argue that black people should have rights. Instead of statues and streets named in Beauregard's honor, I wish that as a girl I would have seen those symbols named after the black people he purportedly had a change of heart about. I wish our teachers had taught us about their lives and accomplishments during and after slavery, during and after Jim Crow. But full-bodied context and historical truth were not academic standards.

When I was born in the seventies, DeRidder had long morphed from a railroad and sawmill town into a paper mill and military one. We lived where most of the black people in DeRidder lived at that time—on the south side of the railroad tracks. Our house was plopped on the southeast corner of Elm and Beauregard Streets. The house's bones were made of pine and covered in aluminum siding that had never been properly painted, and so a white, powdery prepaint substance rubbed off on our skin and clothes when we brushed up against it. Rust the color of dried blood scarred the tin roof.

It was a dilapidated old house, infested with roaches and rats and full of cracks that failed to keep the winter winds out, but Grandmama Avis tried to make it beautiful, to scrape it clean and cozy it up—what with her cleaning sprees at three and four in the morning, her cooking and baking, her quilt making, and her overseeing of the landscaping. She executed such careful shepherding over the little patch of the world she owned, personifying gratitude and dignity.

Even so, the rats and roaches had none.

Their constant scuttling and scratching infuriated me as

much as it disgusted me. In the mornings, our senses were filled with the scent of fresh bread baking and a vat of figs and sugar being cooked for canning, and by afternoon, we were overcome by the intoxication of floured pork chops smothered in Crisco. But by late night, we were taunted by the sound of rat families clawing their way across the insides of our walls and ceilings as we attempted to sleep.

I would lie in bed, my eyes beaming at the ceiling. Indignant and frightened, I wanted to scream out bloodcurdling condemnations that would shrivel the beady eyes and pebble hearts of the rats and set the antennae of the roaches on fire. How dare they tap their disease-infested feet across pots and pans that served us such good food. How dare they lay their translucent roach eggs and push out their measly rat babies. How dare they leave their feces trails in our cupboards like black pepper.

When I think back to our little corner of the universe now, mostly I try to remember the greenery. Plum trees and rose bushes dominated the front yard. Fig trees reigned over the back, pushing their leaves into the clotheslines, providing shade to the garden, and partially hiding the old outhouse that was no longer needed after Papa Houston added a bathroom to the main house.

Growing up, each summer day stretched before us like the stray cats lounging in our neighbor's high grass. In the heat, everything was sticky, including the wooly, circular braided rug in our den, its center gummy with Kool-Aid stains. Our sticky bare feet, caked with dirt on the balls and heels, sometimes caught on tiny splinters in the kitchen floor. For Dena, a tomboy, this setting was a playground. She pulled spider webs from her eyelashes and kept on going, searching for her reflection in the electric-blue eyes of fat horse flies, reaching out her fingers to grab the thin legs of praying mantises, chasing vexed bees and dragonflies, and clambering up trees as though she were born to do so. A patch of woods behind our house beckoned curious children to its cool center, and she and her neighborhood friends would venture into this mini-forest during the heat of the day.

In contrast, I spent the muggiest of days inside reading behind the heavy curtains in the den.

When Grandmama would catch sight of my feet sticking out from under the hem of her curtains, she'd do a double take, especially if the chores had not yet been done to her liking.

"Excuse me, Miss Wonderland, you've got work to do."

But I knew that no matter how much we cleaned, the filth would still be there. The rats would still rattle the walls; the roaches would still drop their eggs like bombs; the braided rug in the den would still be sticky with Kool-Aid stains and whatever spills the generation before mine had made.

"I did clean already," I snapped at her once.

"Oh yeah?" Grandmama responded, just as snappy. "Well, bend your back. Lift the rug." Before I made a move to comply, she bent her own back and lifted up a corner of the rug, revealing crumbs and dirt.

I twisted my mouth.

"Oh, that's nasty to ya, huh?" she said, cocking her head to the side as she took in my expression. She straightened to her full height.

"Lord, I tell you the truth. You wanna be so high and mighty. You want everything so nice and dandy, but you don't clean worth a hill o' beans. You just nice-nasty. That's what you are: nice-nasty."

But wasn't everyone?

Take Papa Houston, for instance. He was so well liked at St. Paul's Baptist Church just down the street where he was a deacon. And as the choir president, he loved to write, rearrange, and sing hymns. His favorite was "No Condemnation in My

Heart." He would sing it so beautifully, so believably, with the organ keys following his tenor's highs and lows. The whole congregation would rise to its feet while the tambourines quivered under all the excitement. I'd watch the tears brimming like crystals in his small eyes, and it was tempting to name them tears of joy.

That is until Papa came home; peeled off his pinstriped church suit; pulled on his old knit pants, plaid shirt, and suspenders; and eased himself down into his worn forest-green leather recliner. He would sit there—no, *sink* there—for hours, drowning in all the memories, the regrets, the longings. For most of his life, he had been a physical man in a physical world. It was when he left the woods that he began to sink into the past. It grabbed him by the waist—a quicksand grip—and would not let go.

As the years wore on, Papa's pants became looser, with his suspenders holding them up the way clothespins grasp the corners of bedsheets, leaving gaps in the middle. Withering away in that recliner, he went over and over the things he had not properly mourned: his marital betrayals, including the one that resulted in a daughter, Emma, outside his marriage; that daughter's early death; the one time Grandmama Avis, in retaliation, stepped out on him; his failure to fix up our sagging house the way he had wanted; and the abuse he had suffered at the hands of his stepfather.

He would chew his gums and think and think, with regret and bitterness coming down like scales over his eyes as he squinted into the past and got caught in its seductive dust: flashes of red swirling inside indigo. He would moan, and he would cry. He would suck his teeth and work himself up into a rage, raving on about how he had raised his fist to a white man once, his shotgun to another. The folds of freckled, reddish-brown skin beneath his eyes would crinkle.

Although armed with only a sixth-grade education, Papa should have been a scholar. He loved to study and compose and read, and Mama says he could perform fractions in his head like nobody's business. Instead, life had assigned him to the lumber mill; he was in his late seventies when cataracts forced him to leave the woods. Grandmama tried to get him out of his recliner to take up gardening, to take daily walks, anything. But building a pantry for our kitchen was the only manual labor he performed after retiring. As he constructed the pantry, I watched his hands gripping the saw as it cut through the plywood, watched the sawdust fall like sand onto the floor.

During his lowest of lows, Papa pined after his daddy, his real daddy, the one he had never met.

"White folks hung my daddy," he would cry. "They hung my daddy before I was even born."

His mother had spent most of her life trying to forget about the past—pushing it down to some place inside her where no one could reach. And yet John, who would father no children of his own, must have known that Burt could never be erased from Mary's heart. Perhaps that is why he would beat Houston mercilessly.

Once when John was not around, Mary, perhaps bent on giving her son something to lift his head, confessed to him that John was not his real father, temporarily consoling his battered spirit as she tended to his bruises.

"His name was Burt Bridges. Burt Bridges, ya hear?"

Burt Bridges.

Houston must have tried out his father's name a million times that day and in the days and years after, feeling the solidity of the *b*'s on his lips before the vowels pushed the sound out and onto the air, ending with consonants—one curt and final, one sliding its way to somewhere else.

"Your daddy was a strong, proud man, you hear me?" Mary

said. "He didn't let nothing break him." But Burt was a ghost father, and whatever she said was not enough for little Houston. His heart ran hot and cold, filling him with chills and fever. With no other stories of his father, his mental picture of Burt Bridges remained one of a body in suspension. His mother never showed the body coming down, and so he kept his father there, dropping into the ears and imaginations of his offspring this same strange image. A dangling modifier in our lives.

"Boy, if I could get my hands around them white people," Papa Houston would say, wringing his wrinkled hands and then dropping them limply. Always, the tears would follow. "I know why Paw beat me so bad . . . it's 'cause I wasn't his real son. I wish I could've known my daddy. I wish I could've just seen him."

Nobody wanted to talk about it; no one wanted to engage the old man in a discussion about the father-shaped hole in his soul—not his mother when she was still alive, not his wife, not Elder Abram down at St. Paul Church who preached about our resurrected savior, our Heavenly Father, but would have been appalled to hear Papa, a saved man, carrying on like that about the fate of his natural father.

Even I, a child who had tried to bury the pain of my own father's absence in my life, judged Papa. What is this, I would think, an eighty-year-old man crying over his daddy? Like the rest of the family, I would pretend to ignore him, refusing to join his pity parties.

GRANDMAMA AVIS SEEMED never to pity her station in life. Instead, she busied herself quilting, cooking, cleaning, and sitting down with neighbors and family members who dropped by unannounced for her listening ear and word of prayer.

She kept her emotions steady, while Papa's rose and fell, rose and fell as he recounted every single injustice that had befallen him. I don't remember Grandmama talking about race at all, although Mama says that during the civil rights movement, Grandmama Avis would pass through the living room as the rest of the family was glued to the television. With her apron tied around her waist, she would occasionally stop and watch the screen for a few beats.

"They can march all they want, and that's a good thing," she said one day. "But this country ain't never gon' be equal. It might get a little better for the black man, but it ain't never gon' be equal."

She donned this attitude of acceptance in all her relationships.

Perhaps Grandma Mary had coached her to leave the past in the past. Avis, whom Mary called "Daught," was the daughter Mary never had, and Mary might have helped fill the hole left by the early loss of Avis's mother.

When she was a teenager, Mama once asked Grandmama how in the world she stayed with Papa Houston all those years, despite his infidelities and rants and even physical abuse that lasted at least until my mother was a young girl. And as I came of age, I would confront my grandmother about handing her social security money over to her youngest son, Billy Joe.

"Why are you always giving him money?" I once asked. "He's just going to blow it on drugs or whatever he does, and he's never going to pay you back. He never does."

"Honey," she said, "love covers a multitude of wrongs." Sometimes she would quote scripture about turning a cheek or forgiving each other seventy times seven.

I stared at the scriptures, trying to imagine forgiving someone once for a grievance, let alone seventy times seven. But Grandmama embodied forgiveness. Still, her stature diminished for me when the white people she had helped raise while she was their parents' maid would visit our home to see her, calling her "Avis," while she referred to them as "ma'am" and "sir" and "miss" and "mister."

I wanted to yell at them, "That's Mrs. Buckley to you! She's your elder. She wiped your butt when you were a baby—how dare you?!"

I wanted to follow Jesus. I did. But the straight-and-narrow path seemed so unfair for my family, who had so little, who had already been through so much. In the Bible, Jesus's words and actions, even his welts of suffering, sounded heroic. On Grandmama, it seemed pacifist, weak, and I could never reconcile her acceptance, her willingness to bury her head in her housework with the woman who at other times stood like an Amazon in my eyes.

The more folks bury a thing, the more they sweep it under a rug, the bigger it becomes, the filthier it becomes—the more it demands to be raised.

To drown out Papa's misery, Grandmama Avis would hum one old spiritual after another, pulling the tunes from deep inside her belly. Sometimes this worked, calming Papa before he got too riled up. At other times, her humming might as well have been a background blues chorus heightening his woes. The louder she hummed—"swing low, sweet chariot . . . God's gonna carry me home"—the louder he got.

Every now and then, she would chide her husband as though he were a child.

"Houston, you've got to learn to forgive. Don't let white folks and all that junk that happened in the past keep you out of heaven. You sit up here all swole up like a toad frog. You need to let that stuff go."

"Hmph," Papa would answer, his chest heaving, refusing to let any of it go.

One morning when she could no longer bear or ignore him, Grandmama lost it. Papa was sitting at the kitchen table where he had finished his grits eons ago. After raging on about some past event, he was spent and sat at the table with his head in his hands, groaning.

Grandmama's tone was stern, quiet, controlled, but with each syllable she uttered, she brought her fist down hard on the iron table.

"Now . . . you . . . look . . . Hous . . . ton."

With her opposite hand, she pointed her long index finger at him from across the table.

"I've had it. Do you understand? I'm not gonna spend the rest of my life around here with you stuck in the past and crying about it."

Taken aback, Papa Houston took in a huge gulp of air, and his chest puffed out like a balloon.

"Well, now, now, now . . . Avis. Now, Avis . . . you don't understand."

"I do, Houston. You think I ain't been through things?"

She had.

She'd survived the death of her mother when she was eleven, her father's molestation after her mother's death, the sight of her mother's ghost slapping her father and forbidding him to touch her again, and her extended family turning on her during the court case that was supposed to try her father but seemed to try her instead.

"Are you saying he put his rod in you?" the judge asked in a tone that humiliated her. "Answer me. Did he put his rod in you?"

She'd survived a stillborn baby and bringing up eight children—through wars, through the Depression, through segregation, through forced integration. She'd survived a philandering husband.

She looked at the shriveled version of the once-strapping

man who had stolen and then broken her heart over and over again.

"I do understand, Houston. But I'm warning you, I'm tired."

But she did not sound tired to me. Her voice was full of its usual strength, but woven within her alto was a faraway quality, as though she had already flown away on the wings of her hymns, fixing her eyes not on the scene before her but on what was unseen, and leaving my papa behind.

I could see her flying away from all of us.

I was standing near the doorway that separated the kitchen from the den, pretending to clean crumbs out of the bread box. Neither Papa nor Grandmama paid me any mind. A few minutes after Grandmama's tongue-lashing, Papa got up and scooted past me, sniffling and gazing at the floor. His chest deflated, he retreated to his recliner.

When he dozed off, I crept up right next to him, took a spot on the rug, and studied his face as he snored. His mouth opened and closed, opened and closed, seeking oxygen. I stared at his toothless gums, losing myself in the sight of all that bare, bare purple flesh.

After days like this, it was better to let him sleep it off and slowly regain his strength to get back to church the next Sunday. Next Sunday, the organist would play, and Papa's feet would get to tapping, and his legs would get to shaking until he shot up to sing his beloved number.

"No condemnation in my heart . . . I got no condemnation in my heart," he would belt out, and the congregation would wish this for him: a clean, clean heart. A light heart. A heart made of feathers. With such a heart, Grandmama wouldn't have to leave my papa. They could fly, fly, fly away together to a place where there would be no more tears, no more bruises, and no more strangely hanging fruit.

DENA WAS SEVEN and I was eight when an unusually frigid winter hit DeRidder. We watched white stuff fall from the sky in hesitant flakes and settle like torn cotton balls against the ground. A thin layer of ice covered the browned grass. I thought of how that ice had choked the green life out of our yard and wondered if the grass would ever be able to revive itself. A row of icicles hung from our low-hanging, lean-to tin roof. Dena said it was all so, so pretty. In my favorite black-and-white horror movies, Dracula's fingers looked like those icicles, long and bloodless.

Grandmama Avis walked into the kitchen and stood over us as we looked out the window.

"Ain't never seen nothing like that before now, have you?"

I shook my head.

"Truth is, the weather's changed patterns over the years. It snowed and iced over like this a bunch of times when your mama was a girl. She and her brothers put thick socks on their hands to keep them warm when they walked to school."

Mama had told us a version of the story before.

"We smeared our faces with Vaseline," Mama said. "When that wasn't enough protection, we walked backward to keep the strongest winds from slicing our faces."

She told us how every day a golden bus filled with white children drove right past her and her brothers, Billy Joe and James, as they walked to school. The bus's tires spewed clouds of snow into the air around them. The children riding the bus would look down at Mama and her brothers. They stuck their heads out the open windows and sang, their voices buzzing like a thousand angry bees: "Nigger, nigger, nigger!"

One day, Mama and her brothers were ready for the bus. They held their heads down so the kids couldn't see their grins. The windows shot up and the kids' tongues pressed against the back of their upper teeth, poised for their vicious chant. Mama,

Billy Joe, and James brought their hands from behind their backs with as much force as they could, slinging rocks toward those scrunched-up faces.

"I tell you one thing," Mama said. "Next time that bus passed us, those windows stayed up and those faces just kept looking straight ahead like they were the ones driving the bus." Mama laughed, and I laughed too, feeling proud. Vindicated.

CORDS THAT BIND

GRANDMA MARY BELIEVED in ghosts. She was always telling of some sighting: a headless man in a powder-blue suit with a hand stretching forth its fingers. Was it Burt paying her visits? Or was it his murderers coming to plead with her?

Walking up to our yard on the way home from school, I would catch sight of her sitting in her usual spot on the porch, spitting snuff into an empty hair grease jar and staring into nothing. Her half-closed eyelids were like the insides of black olives, velvety and moist. Her lips would move, two thin and tremulous things at war with each other. My stomach would sink with knowing: she was at it again.

"There goes a haint," she used to say calmly to noises that seemed, to my untrained ear, like ordinary sounds caused by the wind.

"Get on away from here," she would say to the air. "Get on away from here. Ain't nobody studying you."

I was studying her. My eyes and ears and skin were studying her. Sense recordings stored in the subconscious.

UNLIKE GRANDMA MARY, I'm not sure the disembodied can come back as ghosts, but I do know the past is a ghost. I know that what the captors and lynchers gave us were ghost stories. The omission of records. The uncounting. The three-fifths, or less, of everything. They wanted us to be ghosts: here but not here.

Now they call us delusional. A better diagnosis is that we are the deluded.

I scour books and articles on America's lynchings. Whenever I open the book *Without Sanctuary*, I find it hard to pull myself away from its pages of photographs and stories of men and women who were lynched in this country, some as late as the 1960s. The book consists of reprinted postcards boasting images of men and women hanging from trees, bridges, and poles. The hated skin was stabbed, carved, peeled, and burned. The mobs would keep souvenirs of the mutilated bodies: eyes, genitals, teeth, kneecaps, ears, fingers, hearts. I search the expressions of the white people standing on the ground watching the source of their hatred suspended in air. Sometimes the white people's eyes hold a hollow expression; in other photographs, they are full of smug justification, of joy, if joy can be sullied and smeared and comingled with evil. I see them but cannot hear them.

Each thick page of *Without Sanctuary* takes me back in time with its images presented in black-and-white, sepia, and full color. Pictures of people—of my people—disfigured, grotesque, dehumanized. I wonder if Burt's lynchers stripped him first, or if they let him remain fully clothed; if they stabbed him and burned him or kept his body in one piece. Were the men who stood on the ground staring up at Burt's body wearing vested suits and pocket watches or denim overalls? Were the women smiling into the lenses of cameras? Was the shutter quick enough to capture their souls? Did the little children clutch Bibles? Did they look at the red-rimmed pages of the New Testament and see blood?

What did they want with our Burt? Did they conjure up a rape of one of their white women and try to pin it on him?

We know how obsessed they were with our men's genitals: the black penis—the place of such power and vulnerability. What is this desire to kill what one desires? A public lynching affords the opportunity for a public orgy. Strip him down and behold the captured penis! The mob swells. The mob climaxes with its victim's last breath.

I pray this did not happen to Burt. But that is praying backward, and I am no magician. Still, in my imaginings of him, I always keep him intact. Whole. Dignified.

Burt had a father, a mother, and, perhaps, brothers and sisters.

Consider his mother.

Where was she when they lynched her son? Did she look at the noose around his neck and think of the umbilical cord, that ropelike vessel that had formed inside her to pump her nutrient-rich blood into her baby's abdomen and bloodstream? Mother forming son, two hearts thumping rhythms that became part of each other so that she, even when his heartbeat was no more, could still hear-feel-imagine it?

Here was a world where a woman's body could create a life-carrying cord and white men could tie their man-made rope to a life-giving tree to snatch the life she created away.

Why won't my body cooperate now? she must have wondered.

Why has it forgotten how to give my son life? Why does it not remember how to funnel death's anemic breath out, how to send its waste back into the vacuum of hate from which it came?

Did my great-great-grandmother curse the person who cut the cord binding Burt to her?

BURT, 1904

BURT BRIDGES IS tallying up his first customer of the morning when Sheriff Rogers and two of his deputies walk into his store, shotguns at their sides. The men line up against the back wall in front of wooden shelves full of thick glass jars of fig preserves.

Burt's throat tightens. He draws his attention back to his customer, Richard Handy, who counts out his change while alternately glancing at the men behind him. A few dimes and nickels slip from his sweaty hands and drop to the concrete floor. He nearly falls down attempting to pick them up.

"Calm down, Handy," Burt says, his voice low and steady. "They don't want you."

"Burt, what'd you do?" Handy says, barely moving his lips, his whisper laced with helplessness.

Burt tenses at his friend's question, at the desperation and accusation in it. He licks his thumb and peels open a thin brown paper bag. He places two cans of condensed milk and a jar of coffee into the bag and hands it to the older man, who has been coming to his store every two or three days for the last year.

"What I did, Handy," Burt says, his voice heavy with defensiveness and masked fear, "is stood up for myself."

He grabs Handy's forearm and squeezes.

"I'm going to be fine," he says. "Please. Don't alarm Mary. I'll be home after this is settled." He releases Handy and watches him skitter from his store.

Handy had once owned a small business—a lumber shop. Yet without raising a finger or a word in protest, he had let it go with just a little pressure from town officials. Within days, construction workers tore down his building, the cracked wooden planks penetrating the moist dirt. Mayor Winfrey and his crew had told Handy that they needed his land to build a centrally located hotel, but the real truth, or so the black people in town said among themselves, was that Winfrey couldn't stand to see people stopping by the few colored stores in town to spend their cash. Burt swore he would never give up the little bit of independence his business granted him. He spat on the ground when Handy told him he had settled with Winfrey.

"You buckled under that wisp of a man? How much did he give you, Handy?" Burt had demanded. "What could he give you that you can't make your damn self?"

Handy had hung his head. "Ah, Burt, they was gon' find a way to get it anyway."

Six months after Handy gave up his shop, two men came to Burt with a proposal to buy his land. The message was simple: Mayor Winfrey wanted to sell the area to some developers out of New Orleans. They were looking for cheap land to build a string of resorts where people could come and breathe easier. One of the messengers was tall and lanky and seemed bored with the business talk. He couldn't decide how to hold his arms; he crossed them, let them dangle at his sides, and crossed them again. The second man was short with a pudgy, pinkish face.

"I don't want, and I don't need Winfrey's money," Burt told the men.

"That's *Mayor* Winfrey to you, boy, and you best know this: you making a big mistake," the short man warned him.

"Holmesville is on its way to becoming a major business hub for surrounding counties, maybe even other states. You'll lose this store, sure, but this is for the betterment of the whole community. You can open a store somewhere else."

"You and me both know Holmesville done seen its heyday already," Burt said. "I want my store right where it is, so you tell the mayor to better his town without killing me." Burt picked up a cloth and started polishing his counter, his starched white shirt moving against his olive-brown skin. His gaze fell on the large basket of teacakes Mary baked for the store every morning. Folks said they could find just about anything in Burt's store, but they especially seemed to wake up with the desire for Mary's sweet, powdery biscuits lingering in their throats.

"I won't let my place go for a handful of the mayor's measly money. I won't," Burt said, anger heightening in his voice.

"Burt—"

"No, I say. Now, if you would kindly leave, I've got a store to run."

"You sure are one uppity nigger," the short man blurted out, his face settled into a hard shell.

He swiveled to leave, knocking over an empty kerosene lamp as he made his exit. Burt swept from behind his counter and ran over to the sparkling strips of glass. As he squatted to pick up the larger pieces with his bare hands, the men hopped into the wagon waiting outside. Burt heard the swish of the whip and jumped as it cracked against the horse's hide.

BURT HAD BEEN right about Holmesville. He'd never witnessed its sparkling phase because by the time he'd pushed out of his mama's womb in 1880, Holmesville was already dying, so no one in their right mind could justly blame him—a mere baby, a black baby boy—for its downfall.

As far as towns went, in 1904, Holmesville was still fairly

young. A group of men formed Pike County in 1816 and named Holmesville the county seat. That same year, Chickasaws ceded ten thousand acres in the Treaty of Chickasaw Council House, and in the following year, President James Monroe admitted Mississippi into the Union, making it the twentieth state. After the crowning, people got busy setting up new businesses and shoring up existing ones. In Holmesville, there was E&J Shoemakers, Tessa's Taffy Shop, A&P Grocery, Janice's Dress Shop, a spattering of saloons, and even hotels for travelers stopping in to see what all the fuss over the town was about.

"Oh, how sweet the water is here!" they exclaimed. And it did seem sweeter—with what brought to mind a faint hint of fertile soil and drops of honeysuckle nectar.

Churches sat on corners as churches are wont to do, keeping watch over neighbors, holding secrets and sermons that revealed those secrets to the discerning.

Sheriff Rogers belonged to First Baptist Church on Sugar Avenue but often hid behind his work as an excuse to skip service.

"Well, Sheriff, you the boss. Mightn't you set your own hours down at the station?" Pastor Philips chided him.

The sheriff gave a quick chuckle at the elder man's forthrightness. "I would, Pastor Philips, but you know those deputies of mine can't hardly make up one brain between the five of 'em."

Pastor Philips tried to cover his chuckle with a cough but failed. One of those half-baked deputies was the sheriff's own son, so he dared not add his own two cents.

"How's your missus?" he asked the sheriff, changing the subject.

"Oh, Janice, she's doing fine, doing fine," the sheriff said, his voice trailing off as he glanced just over the pastor's head as though he'd seen his wife walking up behind him.

Born in 1854, Janice Rogers had practically grown up in the shop her parents had named in her honor. During the town's heyday in the fifties and sixties the store had more demands than her parents and their small staff had been able to keep up with. But in 1873, when Janice's parents began shifting more of the weight of running the shop to Janice, their only child, Holmesville lost its reign as the county seat and lost its "cream of the crop right along with it," Janice's father used to say.

When Sheriff Rogers married Janice, they were both in their twenties. He had believed he was marrying into money, what with the family's big white house and its stately white columns that still gleamed in the evening sun. While his in-laws had inherited the home and land, Sheriff Rogers quickly learned that they were just experts in keeping up appearances.

Holmesville had let the family down. And Mississippi had let Holmesville down by changing the county seat to Magnolia. The Illinois Central Railroad tracks were laid west, bypassing Holmesville entirely, and Holmesville's arms were not long enough and its reach not deep enough to hold the interest of developers and politicians for long, and as a result, folks had left in droves.

"Seem like we got more niggers in town than white folks," Janice's father would say to Rogers. "Don't watch it, them blacks'll be tryna take over. They all the time walking by the shop and glancing over like they got eyes on taking it for themselves, Janice tells me. I seen the time when the sheriff would know how to keep his niggers in line."

Rogers had bristled, not with reproach but with defensiveness. He despised the blacks too, but things were different than they were in the older man's day, and he couldn't very well just lynch every black person he saw at will—not without cause.

In 1880, as his father-in-law lay on his death bed, preceded in death by his wife just a year earlier, Rogers promised him that he would see to it that Janice never lost the shop. The more customers she lost though, either through them dying off, moving away, or just not feeling the shop's work was up to snuff anymore, the harder Janice seemed to work. While the number of customers dwindled, so did her staff—until she alone was managing the accounts and the sewing.

"She's so busy I don't even see her much these days," Sheriff Rogers said to Pastor Philips. "Got a few new customers recently."

The pastor nodded compassionately. "That's mighty fine to hear, Sheriff. Mighty fine."

Rogers had walked away from that exchange feeling lower than worms under a rotting log. Not only was he covering for Janice but his own career was also teetering, and he couldn't even let a man of God know they were hurting. He had been forced to lay off most of his deputies, although they still came around to volunteer their services.

At first, the Rogerses blamed themselves (why hadn't they planned better for dire times?), and when that became too much, they turned their eyes outward and saw a town drying up, its once merry streets now graying with negligence. Worry, then fear, then anger ebbed and flowed over the surface of their pupils until nothing was left but rage—solid and silent and hungry.

BURT BRIDGES WAS born and came of age during this period of mass lethargy and resentment in the local whites. Rutherford B. Hayes was finishing out the last year of his presidency, and while some areas in the country were enjoying economic and cultural development, people joked bitterly that they had simply conjured up Holmesville's more prosperous days. Perhaps it had all been a dream—a collective dream. What pained them the most was that they had tasted the potential of progress and now had to read in the papers about it coming to full harvest for other towns.

But Holmesville was only dying in terms of what the white folks in town had grown to love and take for granted, that reigning formula: whites on top (no matter how poor in spirit or assets) and everybody else—blacks and a scatter of remaining native people—on the bottom. The brown folks, on the other hand, were molding a way out of no way in the midst of a failing local economy. Used to the crumbs and scraps blindly falling from the tables of their fairer townsfolk, they were masters at scrounging and saving and scheming. While the white part of town lolled in a drunken, incredulous stupor, crying into moonshine over the town's misfortune, their fellow citizens of a darker hue kept daily life humming—pulling fish from the Bogue Chitto River, hunting, tending farms, helping their bosses run their businesses—and quietly starting their own ventures.

The white residents seemed, to Burt, pathetic and impotent—their only badge of honor the lack of hue in their skin and their glorious past of owning everyone and everything. But where was the honor in that? He didn't share his father's deference to the white man, although his father, from the way Burt saw it, felt an odd kinship with his oppressors, probably given the fact that his father's father was white. Burt could see the Anglo-Saxon lines in his own features, too, despite his darker skin. His father's skin was yellow and pale, whereas Burt's was the shade of hay left out in the sun. Freckles dusted the bridge of his nose like darker spots on a piece of toasted bread. At times, he felt polluted imagining the rape of his great-grandmother, a slave; at other times, he looked at his sharp nose and light eyes and felt he held a secret inside view into his enemy—a view that the white man could never have into him. There was a quiet, inner power in that, and as Burt grew into a young man, he could sense that the white men knew he had something intangible on them, and they didn't like it one bit.

And now, he has given them reason enough to annihilate him, handing his life over like ham on a silver platter.

AFTER THE OFFER to buy his property, weeks passed without a word from Mayor Winfrey's office, and the knots in Burt's stomach softened.

But last night, as Burt was walking home from work, a figure emerged from the shadows, lunging for him. Burt could still feel the skin of the man's neck. He'd grabbed it on instinct. The neck had been like a wet and warm piece of taffy in his hands. It had moved and folded over his fingers. If he had held on a little longer, if he had pressed the flat surface of his thumb closer to the pipe in the man's neck, his life would have disappeared in Burt's hands. But Burt had let go, and the man had run away.

Burt should have run, too, as swiftly as he could in the opposite direction through the forest, across the creek, and to whatever lay beyond. But he had stayed. He had thought that, perhaps, by restraining himself and sparing the assaulting man's life, he, too, could walk free. If the man and his friends wanted to fight him in retaliation, Burt was ready. He would fight them like a man. He'd take a bloody lip home if he had to, but he wasn't leaving or giving up his store. He had a plan, a larger plan, and the store was part of the map to get there.

Mary, who always told him *freedom* was nothing but a word for black folks, had called him crazy and young and foolish.

Mary, you were right, Burt wishes he could say as he stares at Sheriff Rogers and his deputies now. But it is too late.

"You know why we're here, boy?" Sheriff Rogers inches closer to Burt. "Seems you tried to kill someone last night.

Don't you know better than to put your hands on a white man, boy?"

Burt feels the swell of his bladder, a bloating pressing against his belt. He refuses to say anything; there is nothing to say. Whatever would pour from his mouth, he fears, would come out as a plea. "Spare my life," his mouth might say. Or, "Please let me use the john." He imagines the men's laughter over the thunderous sound of his release as they stand with their guns, watching him.

The sheriff beckons the men over to Burt. One man presses the barrel of his gun to Burt's back, between his shoulder blades. The other man lays his gun on the counter, grabs Burt's hands, and ties them together with a short rope. They lead him toward the front of his store, where his periphery catches a bucket of green bell peppers and the "Come Again" sign nailed on the wall to the right of the door.

The men walk through a patch of woods. Burt wonders why they are being so discreet since most lynchings take place in the middle of southern towns where courage builds under the wild eyes of mobs.

The sheriff's hand slackens a bit on Burt's arm, and Burt thinks of breaking from the weak grip. Even with his hands tied behind his back, he could knock the sheriff over with his shoulder or a shocking kick to the back of the sheriff's leg. He imagines himself running a few yards in front of the men; then he imagines the bullets riddling his back, the blood dying his shirt and the back of his head.

The men stop in front of a tree—an oak tree Burt has known all his life.

"Now they won't have to carry you too far to bury you," one of the men says with a sneer.

"Shut up, Frank, and just get on with it," the sheriff barks.

A squirrel stops and stares at the men before zipping away, its narrow body moving up and down, humps merging into each other like waves.

Mary. Burt thinks of the baby growing inside her and hopes that it is a girl. A girl might not find herself hanging from a tree one day. But Mary predicted it would be a boy and had already named him Houston.

"Top of the hill," she liked to say. "Bigger than his daddy's dreams."

My son will never feel my arms around him, Burt thinks. And then, *I will never feel his arms around me*. And then, *I need his arms*.

"But I'm a father," Burt hears himself whispering, a croaking, pitiful sound.

"What was that, nigger?"

"I'm a daddy. I'm gonna be a daddy."

"You shoulda thought of that when you tried to take another daddy's life," one of the men says. "A white daddy."

They all laugh as Burt's body buckles. They jerk him back up.

Burt feels himself separating from himself. He feels another head forming out of his head, its neck stretching itself beyond his neck, and these two heads are fully aware of each other, more alert than Burt could ever be with just one head. These conjoined heads can see all, hear all, smell all. And they are heavy, two giant vessels of intelligence. Heavy and drunk and aware. It is not like being drunk on liquor, though. That kind of drunkenness is a blunt, thick state where one's head wants only a pillow to fall onto and black out. To be drunk in that way is to not sense; it is a burying alive of the senses. No, this drunkenness Burt feels is more like being high off reefer. And the foreign head now looks down at Burt's head and his body with pity and scorn.

"How did you play into their hands?" it asks. "Look at you—another black man going, gone—unable to protect the ones he claims he loves."

A bee buzzes past, free to land on a rose bush. Burt's eyes, the four of them, follow the black body of the bee, its buzzing inseminating itself into both sets of Burt's ears, where the sound amplifies, loud as a motor. Burt's legs try to resist moving. He wants to stop and decipher what the bee is trying to tell him. But the men push on him, drag him, their strength thickened by their numbers and sheer determination and excitement.

I let Mary and the baby down, Burt thinks. And this is how he dies: heavy with duty and doubt and regret. And nature conspires, a passive witness. Who can trust it?

As for the white men, as they lead Burt to the graveyard, to his death over a land of the dead, neon lights flash warnings from the future: this is not the life you want to create for your children and your children's children. Blue, purple, red, yellow, lime—although the visions are shocking, one by one, each man convinces himself that the whirls of light are a figment of his imagination. Not a one of them stops the ship. Not a one of them thinks to say, "This is evil. This is wrong." Each plays his part in the lynching. Afterward, each goes home to his wife and children. Climbs into bed that night. Sleeps as innocent as a baby, cleansed by an internal sense of justification.

But by midnight, shock waves jolt each man awake. Each shoots straight up in bed, blinded by a fusion of electric color. The colors pulsate, stop, and pulsate again, as though they are communicating something. A ring of green light surrounds each man. Still, not a one wakes his wife. They would just as soon step into the green river and be consumed by it than admit their wrongdoing. The ringing pulls each man from his bed and into a forest lit with iridescent flora that is beautiful and frightening, livid and awake with tentacles unfurling and leaves hissing. But it is not time yet for retribution. When the men wake up again, they are in their beds, outwardly unscathed, and maybe their wives know about their sin, maybe their wives sanction it, and when they have sex, their semen is both murderer and life-bringer penetrating their wives' eggs, seeding sons and daughters for generations. They've gotten away with it. Memory washes its hands of it. And not a one of them knows the full force of the forest's threats to them or when it's coming.

Then, as now, the brotherhood remains united. It goes on, acting as both demon and hero. Enduring night after night of hauntings, burying each visitation under the putrid soil of its collective subconscious. Its multipronged tongue is a shovel of lies; its eyes are like Saul's—full of scales and impenetrable pride.

WEAPONIZING TREES

IN MY CHILDHOOD, trees were for climbing and providing fruit and succulent shade. In this way, they were my best friends, alive and silent and strong. Always there, always reliable, even when siblings and friends were not. And so it is with great pain and a sense of betrayal that I look upon the hanging tree.

I want to see the tree that held the weight of Burt's body and the weight of the lynchers' hate—the sin of it. It must have groaned all night after the lynchers exploited its strength to destroy, to kill, to lynch Burt.

As the murderers swung the rope, frayed with dirt, over the tree's fattest branch, as they strung my forefather up by the rope, the tree must have moaned from deep within its belly: "Deliver me! Deliver me! Deliver me!"

It was a futile plea, for it could not uproot itself and flee. And the men could not hear it; their ears and hearts were clogged with spite for the black body before them.

The tree must have tried to will its branches into spears to rain down upon the torturers. And when it failed, it must have envied the willow its thin, wiry, unreliable branches. Was it an oak tree? Yes, it must have been. The oak's strength was its downfall. Its destiny—to remain still and sturdy, to provide covering for man, for beast—was its curse.

It was an unwilling accomplice to Burt's murder, and who

can know how many others? Was it an all-time favorite? Somewhere, in the center of its trunk, lovers from another time, their skin against its bark, carved out a big fat heart with an arrow shooting through it, a heart sandwiched between the names of a boy and a girl, etched for an eternity so that the tree served a dual role: to bring two lovers together forever and to tear two others apart. Forever.

Listen to the oak praying for a tornado powerful enough to uproot its mightiness. Praying for a hurricane to drown it, to wash it of its sins. Listen to it moaning against man, yearning for salvation. For more than a century, beetles have drilled tiny holes into the oak's flesh, releasing sticky tears that drip like molasses throughout the grooves of the bark, spilling over into the limbs of Burt's family tree, but instead of gluing us together, the sap separates. Seals us into isolated pods.

We are a family dismembered, disconnected from its source.

Every year, in remembrance of that day of lynching, all the tree's leaves fall to the ground, attempting mass suicide and failing, attempting to create a map back to the past and failing.

FOR ME, the year 1904 might as well be the dark ages—a period of savagery and ignorance. Intellectually, I know that scores of advances were taking place in technology, the arts, medicine, and education. Some black communities were thriving (before the whites rode in to terrorize and burn them down). When I listen to a piece of classical music from that time, I want to weep. Here is sound that is supposed to symbolize the epitome of class, of refinement, of civilization—and yet my people, in the same moment that a piece of timeless art was being crafted, perfected, and then performed, were treated like animals. I cannot reconcile this primate part of the white man with what he wants me to view him as: better and fully human.

On my desk, I keep a postcard of a black-and-white photograph of an Apache girl taken by photographer Edward S.

60

Curtis in 1904. The child is draped in a blanket, her plump face slightly turned from the camera. Sadness kisses her bronze cheeks; her expressive eyes are brown and wide. In them, I see her ancestors.

Genocide. Slavery. Lynchings. How would I explain this kind of hate to my child? And at what point did I as a child begin to understand it?

IN ELEMENTARY SCHOOL, everything I aspired to had a white face on it. Bionic Woman. Jessica Savitch. Wonder Woman. Barbie. The softly painted women on the covers of my mother's romance novels.

My first best friend was white. Michelle had see-through skin and big gray eyes with specks of green and orange burning from the centers. Little gold hoops glistened against the red of her small ears.

We played together every day in Mrs. Crain's third-grade class; we were, as a pair, loners. No one came near us; we went near no one. We dreamed of growing up and one day marrying Shaun Cassidy or Tom Selleck and of living in a three-story house with gingerbread trimming. As we strolled together on the playground, our shadows followed alongside us, oversized dark copies of our legs cutting across the earth.

One day, I saw Michelle talking to some other white girls. They ignored me when I stood behind her, waiting for her to turn to me, grab my hand, and take off skipping with me down the hallway beyond those silly girls.

Michelle turned around. "Oh."

The other girls looked away. I followed Michelle into the hall. "What's wrong?" I asked.

She dropped her head, her straw hair falling to cover her pink cheeks. "My mom says I can't be friends with you a nymore."

The truth was on the tip of my tongue before it had a

chance to lodge uncertainly within my chest. "It's because I'm black, isn't it?"

Michelle hung her head lower, burdened with something too big, too old, too confusing for her young neck.

I don't know how I knew the answer. I didn't understand. I simply knew.

My friendship with Michelle didn't gradually fade—it stopped abruptly. One day, we were playing together; the next day, I was sitting alone at recess, and Michelle was playing with her new white girlfriends.

On open house night, I searched for the woman who would be holding Michelle's hand. I searched for the woman who had never seen me but hated me so much—who had ruined my recesses.

She was tall and big-bellied and had an unfriendly face framed by bluntly cut chestnut hair. Obsessed, my eyes followed her movements around the room. Trembling, I stared at her chalky skin, at her profile, at her wide back. Her eyes flickered over me coldly as she passed. Michelle stayed stuck to her side. Meanwhile, Mama laughed and talked with Mrs. Crain. She was used to my silences, my deep retreats within myself. She didn't ask me what was wrong, and I would not have known how to find the words to describe to her how I felt: small and ugly, part of a long line of detestable people.

After Michelle, I steered clear of white classmates. In fourth grade, I befriended the new girl that year. Aronna's family had escaped war-torn Laos. We played marbles at recess, united in our otherness. But as Aronna and her family became a more integrated part of the community, she branched outside of our friendship, absorbing into a group of white girls the following school year.

In sixth grade, I befriended the next new student, a tall and fashionable black girl named Melanie. Her mother had moved them back to Louisiana after her marriage to her military husband ended. Melanie, who had been educated in Des Moines, was quickly coined the smartest student in school. She was zany and warm and used her personality to pull a couple more girls into our friendship, including another Melanie and a girl named Loretta, who had deemed me a teacher's pet since kindergarten.

"Remember how you used to bite our fingernails during nap time in kindergarten?" Melanie V. said one day as the four of us sat eating chili corn chips and drinking soda during lunch.

"I remember that!" Loretta said. "But we were too afraid to tell Miss Mims because we knew she would never believe us. She loved you."

Melanie S. bent over laughing. "What was wrong, Sand— were you hungry?"

"I guess so," I said, laughing with them. Their laughter felt warm and inclusive. "And I bet your fingers were dirty. Ew!"

"You still bite your nails," Melanie S. said. "Maybe you ate their nails because you'd already chewed yours up!"

Over the years, I insulated myself with my new black friends in a way that left no room for even the interest of white classmates. Not that any of them were looking my way. Voluntary segregation for us was easy. The norm. Covertly, I noticed Michelle's evolution from the diminutive third grader to the sixteen-year-old cheerleader bouncing through our high school courtyard with boys linked on her arms. When I passed them in the halls, I didn't turn my head away from them; I pretended they were glass—as transparent as the icicles Dena and I had once plucked from our bare fig trees during an icy winter in DeRidder. Fascinated, I had held those jagged jewels of ice up to the sky, gazing at the world through them until they melted into my hand.

THESE ARE THE things I was eager to teach my child: the twenty-six letters of the alphabet, how to count to twenty, how to curl the tongue for the *l* in love, how to read a sentence, a book.

But what is the syntax of racial hate? How does it shape itself into words? Where in the body does it reside, begin to animate itself before it reaches the curl of the upper lip, the knifelike narrowing of the eyes, the flare of nostrils, and the stiff crinkle of the chin? Deeper down the nasal passageway, it steams mucus and then kisses the kidneys, liver, spleen, and intestines with gaseous toxins. Along the spine, it climbs, forcing each bracket of bone straight. Even the curve in an old woman's spine stands up to help her fill her esophagus with spittle to spew a nasty word at the black man waltzing down the sidewalk, dressed in his Sunday best and with the nerve to keep his head held high as he approaches her. Her own stockings are tattered. Her leather purse hanging from the crook of her arm is empty save a couple of soft peppermints; a letter from her son who has moved so, so far away; and a handful of coins.

Still, she deems herself superior to the nigger. Hate whispers such sour nothings in her ear. It emboldens her. She spits in his black face.

What mother—then or now—can prepare her child for the curled tongue of someone's hate?

BEFORE MY PREGNANCY, I had never been to the doctor for anyone but myself. I found it strange to be sitting in an ob-gyn's office surrounded by family and parenting magazines. I would pick up magazines where "8 Ways to Raise a Brain-Fit Baby," "Perks of a Summer Bump," and "Get Her Glow" were the dominating cover teasers. One day, a woman sat in the corner farthest from me, one baby in a bassinet and a toddler climbing over her thighs. The toddler pressed her finger to her mother's nose.

How cute, I thought, but the mother's expression remained unmoved, her face unlined by annoyance or entertainment.

In another corner, an older kid played two noisy toys simultaneously—a plastic xylophone and a Baby Einstein that spoke in Spanish, French, and English, or it would have if he had allowed the thing to keep speaking. Instead, he kept pressing the button before the voice could finish each word—*turtle*, *starfish*, *piano*. He switched frantically between colors and animals. It set my teeth on edge; the nerve endings in my gums and along my arms frizzled, and I remembered a promise I made to Marcus: I will never scream at our child. But my mother was a yeller, and I could feel her frustration rising on my tongue as I shifted in my seat away from the annoying sounds. I made a new promise: at least, I will never spank my child. To be safe, I added, at least I will not whip my child like I was whipped: with plum-tree switches.

I know what it's like to be whipped, switched. To have the trees I so loved and ate from turned against my flesh, drawing blood and welts and tears. This is the effect of the trauma of slavery. Things hold. For me, the tree branch, especially, was the most humiliating and frightening form of punishment. And having to go outside to get your own weapon—that was a torture chamber hall stretching into eternity. Being sent back to get a more ferocious switch because the first paled in comparison to the switch in your mother's imagination—well, that was reason enough to ask the trees to bury me.

The art of torture is a thing passed down. John Buckley beat Mary and Houston, and while I am inclined to romanticize Mary, the truth is that she was later guilty of brutally beating one of her grandsons who lived with her and John for a time. Papa Houston grew into a man who beat his wife. Mama remembers running after him one day as he was running after her mother. Being a young girl, she thought it was a game.

"What are you doing daddy? I wanna play!"

Her mother was cornered and cowering. My mother saw her father's arm raise in the air with his fist balled; she saw the rage on his face. What had angered him?

"He was complaining about the pastor, and Mama had simply said, 'Well, Houston, why don't you go down there and talk to him?'" Mama recalls. My mother's presence at the scene that day spared Grandmama Avis the full measure of Papa Houston's wrath. He came to himself when he heard his daughter's tiny voice, confused and questioning. His rage melted into shame. We carry each other's fear and shame and pain.

I will never forget what plum-tree switches feel like against my skin.

By the force of the switch's stings, I could tell if Mama was angry at something bigger than us, or if she was angry with the world. I had not killed anyone or stolen money from anyone or raped anyone. I had not cursed or spat in anyone's face. What was the offense—not washing the dishes? Rolling my eyes? Whatever it was, the force of the stings did not match my crime.

The cells on the inside of the tree pressed against the cells on the inside of our legs, arms, and backs. What if the skin breaking on the limb broke the membranes in both the tree and the girl? What if our protoplasm mixed, milky fluids of tree and human life? Part of our DNA is wrapped up in the DNA of the tree that was forced to swallow Burt's life and maybe that is what the switchings really were: an unconscious reminder. We are bridges made of blood and water, soil and skin.

"The Bible tells us to spare not the rod," Uncle Junior used to preach, but I don't think it meant for us to be beaten with things that are still alive.

FAMILY REUNION

I PROMISED MYSELF that after the baby was born, I would visit the land Mary and Burt knew. Even if I saw no live human bodies, I knew the trees would still be there—the dirt, the grass, and the remains underneath.

And I would listen for their whispers of truth.

I wrote the state of Mississippi to request a death certificate for Burt. In most of the slots on the request form, I had to write "unknown" or "possibly" or "in or around." Per the state's request, I made a photocopy of my driver's license, musing on the privilege of information, of being "known" with my recorded birth date, address, height, weight, a photograph, and the fact that I need corrective lenses. Numbers are assigned to me. I am accounted for. My child, grandchildren, and great-grandchildren will be able to prove that I existed.

Mississippi wrote me back quickly:

We have been unable to process your request for the reason or reasons stated below. The law requiring the filing of death records with Mississippi Vital Records became effective November 1, 1912. Since the records requested by you are prior to that date, they are not available. You may, however, wish to contact the Mississippi Department of Archives and History, which may be able to assist you in locating other records of interest.

They enclosed the seventeen-dollar check that I had sent to

them, yet seeing it sitting there on top of the impersonal letter made me feel like Mississippi had stolen something from my family all over again. But what had I expected? A phone call, a personal letter? An apology?

I was nearly one hundred years and two thousand miles away from the flesh-and-blood Burt Bridges, but my skin had touched the skin he loved, the skin that loved him, and therefore, I knew he had lived and breathed and loved.

I folded Mississippi's letter and sat down to write the state of Louisiana for Mary's death certificate since her birth certificate would not be available in Mississippi either.

THROUGH AN ONLINE newspaper service called Newspapers.com, I found old Mississippi newspapers published around the time Burt and Mary lived in or near Pike County. Tiny blurbs about lynchings are tucked in between reams and reams of type. These crumbly mentions hold no outrage, no investigations. That work was left to someone whose very life was also threatened, Ida B. Wells, who was forced to fill in the gaps, to humanize, and tell the story of the horrors of lynching when many of her white journalist counterparts were justifying it. The following excerpt, published in the *Macon Beacon* in 1904, is from an editorial writer who fancied himself charitable toward the American Negro and in the very same mind and heart, with even more intensity, endorsed the "extermination" of the entire race:

> The negro is increasing in criminality. Liberty is regarded by him as a license. The only remedy is restraint and the enactment of laws to suit his peculiar mental and moral nature. Laws suited to the white man do not fit the negro. The fifteenth amendment of the Federal Constitution should be repealed. It would be the best thing that could be done for the negro. Indeed, it would be his salvation. It will afford him protection

and secure his rights as a negro. I am the negro's friend. I believe in protecting him in the pursuit of happiness and the enjoyment of the products of his labor. But I am opposed to him voting and anything that savors of social equality is repulsive. I believe he should be given instruction in the schools which will develop his moral nature and educate his hands to perform profitable labor. A backward glance at history and a profound study of the Anglo-Saxon race emboldens me to say that in spite of constitution and laws, the white man will not share in sovereignty and dominion with the black man. And when the black man undertakes to force a division of authority, there is going to be trouble and then the ultimate extermination of the black man. The picture is a gloomy one, but facts are inexorable and we cannot escape direful consequences by covering our heads in the sand drifts of error or resorting to a policy of doing nothing. The occasional murder, raping and mobbing which ruffle the serenity of the public mind today are but the premonitory symptoms and fore runners of the storm which lurks behind the horizon of a few decades.

Around the same time, the *DeSoto Times*, a newspaper in Hernando, Mississippi, published the following:

Whitecaps are attempting to terrorize a negro in Pike County because the negro has been industrious and has purchased some land. An attempt is being made to bring the Whitecappers to justice.

An attempt? Who was making the attempt? How strong or feeble was it? And who was the "industrious" negro? Could it have been Burt?

FORTY-FIVE YEARS after his father was lynched, Papa Houston endured a kind of lynching trial that his family feared would end with the loss of his life—either behind bars for life or worse.

On a Sunday afternoon in 1949, Houston drove his car down a narrow dirt road that snaked in between fields of vegetation on either side. Whenever he had a free day now and again, Houston loved to take his family on long drives through the countryside. They had left DeRidder behind more than two hours earlier, heading north with no particular destination in mind.

Avis sat in the passenger seat holding their sixth child, James. It was just the three of them. The other boys were young men already. The first cluster of them had already gone out on their own, while the two still at home were itching to follow and put their stamp on the world.

Houston glanced over, catching a small frown on Avis's face.

"Lady, what's wrong with you?"

"Oh nothing," she said, and smiled at him. The wind carried the faint scent of pine into the car. Avis breathed it in and brought her hand to rest on Houston's knee. "Nothing at all."

A few miles away, a pickup truck was barreling down a side road. The woman inside the pickup pleaded with her husband to slow down, but he had been drinking since morning, and his head was swollen with stubbornness even on sober days. He looked at his wife and bared his teeth at her. Her passenger window was rolled down but the thick, putrid air inside the truck still choked her.

"Let down your window," she begged her husband.

He said nothing.

Seconds later, she was screaming but not because he had ignored her.

"You're going to hit those people!"

It was too late.

Their truck slammed into Houston's car, a frightening sound, followed by silence. The baby tumbled out of Avis's arms; his cries came quickly and then stopped. Avis examined him, but he was more startled than hurt. She rocked him back and forth and turned to see Houston's forehead littered with tiny cuts. She couldn't get her insides to stop quivering, but her legs still worked.

"You guys all right?" Houston asked.

"Yeah—you?"

"I'm okay." Avis went to touch his forehead, but he pulled away. He opened the door and stumbled from the car. Holding James tightly, Avis followed suit.

Shattered pieces of glass glinted against the crushed hoods of the truck, the car, and the road. Avis listened closely as a low wail punctured the air over and over again.

She saw a white woman rubbing her stomach and staring blankly at the ground, but her mouth was closed. Avis walked away to investigate the source of the sound; it filled and emptied her. With James holding tight to her shoulders, she dragged her feet closer to that awful wailing. It was rising from a shallow ditch on the side of the road. She looked down.

A man was flat on his back in the trench.

Her gaze penetrated the thin layer of blood: the man's face was gone.

Glass—or metal—had peeled the skin right off. Pieces of it hung from his scalp, but his face was gone. There was nothing but yellowish fat, muscle, and the whites of his rolled-back eyes.

When the deputies arrived, the man was dead. They turned to Houston, handcuffed him, and charged him with manslaughter.

And Avis thought to herself, *They mean murder*. Because to slaughter a man is to murder him, no matter which way you turn it.

The new widow spoke up. "That man didn't kill my husband," she protested, shaking her head, her cry as shrill as a hawk's. "My husband—he'd been drinking all day. He ran into those people."

The deputies looked at each other.

"Ma'am, don't you worry yourself any," one of them said. "Everything will be taken care of."

The woman strained against the deputy's arm as she turned to watch Houston being led away from his family.

In the hour before Houston's trial for manslaughter started, Avis saw the widow sitting on a bench in the hallway. She glanced at her, catching the faraway look in the woman's eyes as she stared right through her. Avis's stomach sunk as she wondered if the deputies and attorneys had gotten to her. Would she tell the truth like she had at the scene of the accident? In the middle of mud and broken glass and new death, the truth had been expelled from her, but with some passing of time, had truth had time to cool off? Backtrack?

Avis was hit with a sudden sorrow for the woman. She wanted to go to her and tell her, "I am sorry you lost your husband." But she couldn't—not before she was sure the white woman wasn't going to be the cause of her losing her own husband—her children's father.

When the widow took the stand, she sat as straight as a side of plywood in the chair. Her fingers were laced together. She wore a mint-green nylon suit (something to keep her nerves calm). Her lipstick was as bright peach as the roses in Avis's front yard, as was the matching rouge lifting her cheeks. Her frizzy dark-orange hair, which had been all over the place on the day of the accident, was smooth, glossy, and held down with bobby pins.

In a small but clear voice, she relived the accident calmly. Her report was factual, almost like a robot, clearing Houston of blame.

She had chosen everything carefully for this trial—her clothing, her mannerisms, and her tone of voice, but none of that mattered as she blinked rapidly at the angry accusing eyes of the prosecutor standing before her.

Avis could see it in the jurymen's eyes, feel it in the air in the courtroom: they were going to railroad her husband. The same fate that had befallen his daddy had raised its ugly head to haunt him some forty-odd years later. Would these men, protected by their uniforms and the law, lynch Houston too?

In the courtroom, the white woman was the only witness of value. Who had her husband been? A man of political standing? A hardworking father? A shiftless man with a long record of drunk driving and petty crime?

"My husband . . . he was sloppy drunk, Your Honor. He'd been drinking all day. I begged him . . . I begged him not to get behind that wheel."

"Your husband is dead, ma'am," he yelled back at her, as though trying to shake some sense into her. "Are you telling me—are you telling these gentlemen of the jury—that your husband knowingly ran into this"—he spun his head around—"nigger's car and killed himself?"

The woman's face tightened, and the tears she had been clamping down overcame her.

Her nylon skirt shifted against the wooden seat as she twisted away from the men of the jury, away from the attorney. Her wet, exasperated eyes sought out the judge, whose face was set in stone. Weariness slogged in the widow's throat, but her words were clear.

"My testimony stands, Your Honor. This man, Mr. Buckley, is innocent."

Those white folks—the lawyers, the jurymen, and even the judge—mewled around for a while longer after that, contradicting each other, scratching their heads, throwing their weight around, but in the end, the only folks who had actually witnessed the accident were the two families involved. As Avis sat in the back, worrying a handkerchief, she might as well have been invisible. But the good Lord shone a ray of light in the courtroom that day, and as she watched that light cut through the room, it calmed her. In the end, the judge and jury determined that Houston was innocent.

The deputies had to unlatch the handcuffs around the black man's wrists. Avis's knees buckled under her as she stood up. She had caught hold of the back of the bench in front of her to keep from falling—that's how shocked she was at the verdict. Out in the hallway, Houston's older boys squeezed their daddy tight, and Avis turned her head from the sight of them to keep herself together.

They never saw the widow again, although Avis often wondered what happened to the woman. They went back to DeRidder and never drove through that part of the state again. Houston and Avis went back to their lives, working and taking care of the kids. Avis birthed Billy Joe and my mother over the next couple of years. One midnight when she was knee-deep in washing the children's clothes after working all day cleaning and taking care of her boss's house and little ones, something dawned on Avis: "It sure would be nice to get out of here and take a drive. Just get away from it all."

They hadn't taken one of their leisurely drives since the accident a few years before. She brought this up to Houston the next morning, but he dismissed her.

"We ain't got time to be driving around this godforsaken state going nowhere fast." He tried to sound aggravated, but his voice trembled just enough for his wife's ears to pick up on it.

Houston had been let go that day in the courtroom, but he hadn't been freed at all.

MY INITIAL QUEST to uncover and knit together the pieces of my family's story began in 2001, five years before I became pregnant. I was still married to Ric, a New Yorker I had met in 1995 in New Orleans, where we both worked as journalists for the local daily newspaper. While we loved New Orleans, we believed we could expand our professional horizons in Los Angeles, where he landed a position as a staff photographer for the Associated Press, and I was accepted into a graduate program for writing.

A month before Ric and I left Louisiana, my family hosted its first-ever reunion. I drove from New Orleans to DeRidder with the now late musician and composer Harold Battiste, who had also become my friend after my writing mentor introduced us to discuss Harold's desire to write a memoir. The trip to DeRidder was especially magical for Harold: in the 1950s, the segregated high school George Washington Carver High, my mother's high school, had given Harold his first job out of college. He taught music there and started the town's first band for black students. Going back to DeRidder was a full-circle moment for him as he reflected on his music career, as well as other personal life choices he'd made during that time.

My motivation for going was twofold. I was excited to see family members I had not seen in a few years, and I also viewed the trip as an opportunity to begin understanding my family history as ground zero for analyzing an emotional encounter I had the previous fall while on a trip to New York with Ric.

Ric was born at Harlem Hospital on a cold January night in 1958. Except for a brief stint in the army, he had lived in New York City for most of his life. In his late thirties, he moved to New Orleans to take a job as a photographer at the daily newspaper about a year before I was hired.

Before moving to New Orleans, Ric told his New York and New Jersey journalist pals, "If I come back with a twang, shoot me." He didn't realize there are various dialects in the South, that folks in parts of New Orleans sound like Brooklynites. He certainly hadn't banked on marrying a southern girl after nearly making it to forty without ever committing to a long-term relationship.

Northern boy and southern girl. Child of the great black migration and child of the ones who stayed.

In October of 2000, he took me to his home city, and it was everything I had grown up imagining.

"I love New York," I told Ric as we walked down 125th Street during the warmest part of the afternoon.

"Beautiful!" I yelled as he zipped past me on his rollerblades in Central Park.

Later that evening, we explored Fifth Avenue on foot, and my excitement began to wane as the sun retreated.

"We can't move here though," I said to his back as he strode ahead of me. "It's too cold, and you're walking too damn fast."

"Oh, come on, it's just a little cool," Ric said without slowing his pace. He was back in his element.

By nightfall, the city's temperatures were dipping into the low thirties, yet in spite of the weather, I wanted to experience the nightlife, to peel off coats and scarves, to dance and sweat and dance some more. On the subway, I flipped through the pages of the *Village Voice* and came across the description of a nightclub that coined itself as hot and soulful.

"You ain't gonna be able to pull me from the dance floor tonight," I said as we got off the train and walked to his mother's apartment in Washington Heights. "I need this."

"You need it, huh?"

"Yeah, I need it. I need to dance. I've been eating like a hog here. And anyway, if I gotta shake in this doggone city, I want to be responsible for some of it."

"Wow, you sound country."

"You ain't but one removed from the South your damn self." My chin, my lips, my nose were wrapped in a thick chenille scarf the color and texture of moss, and my voice came out muffled. "You know your mama didn't leave all her ways in South Carolina."

At his mother's apartment, we ate a dinner she had prepared for us, then got dressed to go out.

On the subway, I waited until we were close to our stop in Greenwich Village before easing a plum gloss over my lips.

Ric watched me as I frowned into the compact mirror. "You look fantastic," he said.

"Really? I look okay?"

Ric looked at me with softened eyes.

"How many times do I have you tell you, Sand? You're beautiful."

I snapped the compact closed and beamed at him. "You're the one who's beautiful."

We got off the subway at Astor Place and walked four blocks. As we rounded the corner and drew near the line outside the club, I nudged Ric. I was shocked to see a string of white people waiting to get in.

"Looks like we're the only black people here, babe."

The blurb in the paper had definitely said, "Live DJ playing R&B and hip hop."

We had fled New Orleans, that mostly black city, to get away from our oppressive, mostly white work environment. We had promised not to speak of the editor who narrowed his blue eyes at me and made crude jokes about black and Latino students; the photographers who believed Ric's appointment had blocked other white photographers from that opportunity, even though Ric was one of just two black photographers on a hefty staff; and the reporters who spent their time gossiping, tearing apart other writers' stories behind their backs and complaining about affirmative action just because, every purple moon, a black reporter was hired.

"I don't know, Ric." My words were slow and careful, but I followed in his footsteps. "I don't feel like partying with just white people. I really want to have fun. I really want to dance."

"Well, we're here now," Ric said as I shivered a few feet behind the last person in line. "Maybe we should go in and get out of this weather. Let's just go in and have fun. At least we're together."

I twisted my mouth to one side. "Sure we can't find another place around here?" I wanted to look upon other black women, see their outfits, and study their hairstyles. I wanted to relish other black men's silent appraisal of my looks while pretending not to notice. I wanted the men and women to acknowledge Ric and me on the dance floor, to marvel at the energy that I hoped would shimmy between us.

I tried again to sway him.

"We could go find a paper and look for something else. Maybe that reggae place in Brooklyn that you read about."

"Really?" he said. "You really want more walking? More subways?"

He's right, I thought. Why should we be the ones to leave while they use our rhythm and our blues as their entertainment?

"You're right, Ric. Let's just see. If we don't like it, we can leave. Besides, maybe the black people are already inside where it's warm."

We went in and there were white people everywhere. In feathers and furs and striped tights, in wigs and fake eyelashes and glitter. I had forgotten it was Halloween. We walked upstairs to the coat check where there was another dance floor with the same scene.

"Do you want to leave?" Ric asked after looking around.

Now it was my turn to be practical. I reminded him that we'd paid twenty bucks apiece to come in here.

"Maybe it'll get better," I said.

A black DJ with skinny, jaw-length dreadlocks played a mixture of house music and hip hop. The dance floor, packed with gyrating pelvises, moved like one big undulating response to his calls.

All of my desire to dance had drained.

"Do you want something to drink?" Ric asked me more than once. "Do you want to dance?"

"No."

The minutes dragged on, an hour. My immobility kept Ric frozen to a spot in the corner of the club.

"You've spoiled what could have been a perfectly good night," he said, finally, frustrated.

My arms were locked across my chest. We were standing against a wall by the ladies' room. The long line of alcohol-filled women waiting outside the door was not moving.

"Sand, we're here now. I am begging you, why can't you just try to have fun? Forget about them. We're here to enjoy each other and the music. These white people have a power over you. They're in here having fun, and look at you. You're not hurting them; you're hurting us. They couldn't care less."

And that's the problem, I thought, but I kept my lips clamped.

The women standing in the bathroom line were giggling and gossiping and straining to hold in their pee. They seemed so free, so confident, and so unbound by anything. So privileged. The inside of my nostrils grew moist and stinging as though I had inhaled spray from an onion. Through this wetness, I breathed, "I hate those stupid bitches. I just hate them."

Ric coughed out an incredulous, joyless laugh. He ran a

hand over his closely shaven head as he tried to smooth patience into his voice.

"Sand, the white people in this club have done nothing to you. You can't hate all of them because of what some of them do. White people are a fact, babe. They will always be in power in this country. You're either going to learn to live with them, or you won't get too far."

I wanted to hurt him for speaking the truth and making me hurt, for making me feel powerless and outdated and unsophisticated—so 1980s or '60s or '50s. I wanted to hurt him for being so adaptable. Ric, who had at times seethed with hatred for whites too. Ric, who had, because of his experiences with many of them, made generalizations about the entire race too. Still, he had been able to embrace some white people as true friends—and as lovers. I hated him for that part. I wanted to suck the life from him—all his reasoning and maturity and acceptance.

I was six months away from turning thirty, and I had not made any close white friends and had never dated outside my race.

My eyes drifted from the women and returned to Ric's face. "Oh, I can take them in doses all right." My voice was a low, slow growl. "But—unlike you—I don't want them in my bedroom."

Ric's nostrils swelled before he pushed his long, thin face to mine; his shiny near-black skin darkened to purple underneath. His pupils glittered like a piece of granite in the sun, growing harder and blacker.

"Like I told you before," he said, his enunciation sharp, "I do not have to justify my past to you. I don't have a problem with white people who don't have a problem with me. You have no right to judge me. No right."

He straightened to his full height. His eyes moved from me

to the line of women outside the bathroom and then back to me again. "You've got a real problem, Sand. A real problem, and you need to get help."

Tears and makeup slid down my cheeks and over my collarbone, which was so bony it protruded almost abnormally from my chest. Was he tender when he kissed white women there? I yearned to be kissed on my collarbone, to feel the hard smoothness of his teeth sinking there into my skin, underneath my bone.

Ric looked at me with disgust.

"Let's go."

Upstairs, Ric jerked on his jacket. I wanted to take everything back. I wanted to go back to that corner at Astor Place before we turned and saw the club. I wanted to keep walking confidently arm in arm with Ric and to make a small joke about being the only black people in the place. I wanted us to acknowledge it, shake our heads, and wonder where the black people were partying tonight but keep it moving.

"We're going to have fun here," I'd say. And we would.

I wanted to take it all back. But I could not take any of it back.

It had not started there, in that dark, pumping club.

It had not started on that corner.

It had not started that night.

ON THE DRIVE from New Orleans to DeRidder, I thought of the night in New York and wondered what my family would think of my experience in the nightclub with Ric. Was I the only one with deep-rooted hate and insecurities? I had never spoken in depth with any family members about race.

The family reunion would stand as a living testament of the labor and love that Grandmama and Papa had invested in the family. Grandmama Avis, Papa Houston, and two of their sons,

David and Billy Joe, had died in the 1990s. We living relatives were tired of returning to DeRidder and reuniting only as the result of a loved one's death. So this time, we returned to celebrate life—to be joyous, not mournful.

My cousin Tessie and I first started talking about planning a reunion a couple of years earlier. We would call each other on our employers' phones, hunched over in our cubicles, whispering into the receivers. Our calls simply sprinkled the seeds. She lived in Houston, and I lived in New Orleans then; our footwork was nonexistent. It was our relatives who still lived in DeRidder who brought the reunion to fruition.

We gathered at the Masonic Hall, a metal, tent-shaped building on Beauregard Street. As Harold connected with my family and reconnected with a former student, now an elder herself, I was glad that I had not had to attend the event alone. Still, a part of me longed for my husband and extended family to meet, but he refused to make the trip because he did not like my mother. She had been dismayed that I was marrying an older man, and he had not taken kindly to her barbs.

In the 1980s, the Masonic Hall was one of the buildings my family used to rent for church services. The building was drab, always cool and dank inside, yet we would warm it up with singing and drumming. Dena and I were pros on the tambourine. Leaving the flat-palmed beating to the adults, we competed with one another, flipping our right wrists vigorously and shaking the tambourines in the air before bringing our opposing palms to dance all over the instruments' skin.

Mama would pick the strings of her white and silver Peavey guitar, and the sound bursting from the amplifier bounced off the concrete floor, sending tremors through our bodies. As my cousin Buck beat his drums, hitting the cymbals lightly, Mama's fingers would curl even deeper into the guitar's strings, and she would sing "Like a Ship . . . (Without a Sail)" in her sharp, cracking lilt with her head bent sideways and tears streaming down her face.

At the family reunion, she played her newest guitar, a flashy emerald-green-and-blue Fender, while my uncles strained their aging vocal cords in once-popular gospel quartet songs, and the little children, my second and third cousins, laughed and clapped with joy.

While I watched from the sidelines as relatives celebrated life, something was missing. I sat down at an old classroom desk next to the door and wrote down the names of relatives as they strolled in. Each time I wrote down the name Buckley, I thought not of John Buckley, but of Burt Bridges. I wanted, even then, to dismantle the family's adopted name, to abate my younger relatives' ignorance.

I started asking some relatives if they had heard the story of Burt Bridges, but they looked at me with confusion. They wanted sweet tastes in their mouths, music in their ears, and fond moments that would grow into memories. There was no place for my sketchy and depressing genealogy report. Besides, I had allowed distance and years to estrange me from most of my cousins. Why, they may have wondered, was I obsessing over someone long dead, someone they had never heard of? After a while, I left my post at the door and walked over to a group of cousins.

"Where's your hubby at, Sand?" my cousin Thurman asked.

"Oh, he's working," I said. "And packing for our move to Cali."

"Y'all still haven't made any babies, huh?"

"We don't want children, silly," I said.

"Mm-hmm," he said, looking pointedly at my yellow sleeveless dress, which clung to my abdomen and hips before flowing out to my ankles.

He turned to his audience.

"I know why Sand don't wanna have kids, y'all. She don't want to lose that girlish figure."

"You're a mess," I said, laughing and turning away.

I walked away from Thurman's discussion about my waist-line and headed toward my uncles.

Uncle Herbert, my eldest uncle, tall and square faced, sidled up to me and laid a heavy hand on my shoulder.

"So, you and your husband are getting out of Louisiana for good, huh?"

"Yes, sir, we are," I said.

Uncle Herbert put his free hand over his wide chest. "Sand, I have to tell you, baby—I get real shaky in here whenever I hear about somebody moving out to California. Real shaky."

"I'm trying not to think of the earthquakes, Uncle Herbert. New Orleans has its hurricanes, besides."

I forced myself to look into his eyes. As he held my gaze, I wondered if he thought I should change my plans. What was he most afraid of?

Years earlier, when I was just a girl, Uncle Cricket had prophesied my leaving.

"I had a dream, Sand," he'd said, "that you were standing there in that doorway like you doing now, and then . . . you was gone."

His dream had been unsettling to me: Was I gone because I was dead or had I merely grown up and moved away? And which was worse?

During the Great Migration, most of my family, with the exception of a few stints in the military, had remained in the South. Was he trying to warn me that it was too late to migrate? After all, reverse migration, a back-to-the-South movement, was in effect, with black families flocking back to the values they had once fled, where new opportunities had arisen, and the village was still needed.

Now it was Uncle Cricket who saved me by shifting the focus away from my relocation plans.

"Don't listen to my brother with all that talk," he said. "What I want to know is this." He paused and offered a full grin. "When are you going to write that book about the family?"

"Don't worry. I'm working on it, Uncle Cricket," I said, one generation's pledge to another, flowing backward.

Uncle Herbert looked from his brother to me with a wide, sparsely toothed smile as if to say, "Nobody told me about this."

"Good," Uncle Cricket said. "Call me anytime when you get to California to ask me anything, and if I don't know the answer, I'll try to find it out for you."

He elbowed me and leaned close to my ear as though guarding a secret only he and I shared. " 'Cause you know there ain't really anybody here who's got the answers."

He pulled back and gave me a wink.

I left DeRidder full of determination, buoyed by Uncle Cricket's encouragement.

That determination waned over the years, but budded again in 2006. I linked our ancestor's aborted promises to my own, a kind of quantum entanglement. I attempted to erase the distance between us, the years, the laws of physics and of man—just papery things really. I'd seen my share of time travel flicks, and it seemed plausible. Scientists say we are not matter but energy. A sheet of paper turns out to be a magic carpet after all, so I hop on, riding its electric waves through time.

DEAD ENDS

I WAS ELEVEN when Grandma Mary died, but I do not remember her funeral or burial. Perhaps we kids did not attend. My mother is the keeper of some records—deeds to the old Elm Street house, her parents' delayed birth certificates—but she possessed no copy of Grandma Mary's obituary or death certificate—no paperwork proof of her death and, therefore, life.

It was not until I was on the verge of motherhood in California that I wrote the state of Louisiana to request her death certificate, desperate to have something officially tangible of her existence. Something that I could point to and say, *This was Grandma Mary.*

I wanted it because I believed there might be a kernel of a clue that could unlock some part of the mystery that was her life. Shortly after Grandma Mary died, I was snooping around in Grandmama Avis's room and found a severed lock of braided hair, silver with speckles of black, stuffed inside an envelope. Was it Grandma Mary's? As a kid, I was always playing the sleuth. I was both fascinated and frightened by the feel of her braid, the texture of which remains imprinted on my fingertips. What was this lock of hair supposed to tell us? Who had cut it from her head and why?

I do not know what happened to the braid in the years since my discovery. Someone's attempt to hold on to an external symbol of her, an external piece of evidence that she had, indeed, existed, is now also gone. In all my scattered looking for Burt, I began to realize that Mary, too, has been nearly erased.

WHEN I DREAM of Mary, she is a young girl, not the old woman I once knew.

Her face is a wilting flower inside a full moon, purple bud pulsing, fading. Her fingers are the legs of a miniature ballerina, and her convex nails are the ballerina's pointed and satin-skinned feet.

I look upon her uncratered face, her penetrating blackbird eyes, and her beautiful unlined fingers kept warm and delicate by the blood in her heart, and wonder how can there be blood, considering she has been dead for so long.

Angry, I look back at her face with accusing eyes: "How can you be alive?" I scream. "Why won't you speak?"

Unmoved by my passions, she stares straight at me, the surface of her face turning a cool gray, freezing the flow of my blood that is also her blood.

MARY, 1904

BY LATE MORNING, Mary is at the tail end of her chores. She has fed the chickens and groomed her two mules, Maul and Betty, and now she is washing the laundry: one hand holds a lye-filled piece of clothing while the other holds a washboard. As she beats and drags each cloth over the washboard's ridges, the baby inside her kicks incessantly. Mary stops for a moment to catch her breath.

"How them lil' legs of yours get so strong all of a sudden?" she says, looking down at her belly.

Even pregnant, Mary prefers working outdoors over domestic work indoors. She will keep tending to her small crops until the baby is ready to drop. She will never work as a maid, not even temporarily. She hates the dust that accumulates in corners and the spider webs hanging from places people don't want them hanging. She especially hates dealing with human waste.

"All them white ladies want is for you to carry around they slop jars all day so they can perfume themselves all up and pretend to be pretty powdering their noses," she told Burt once. "What those noses need is to smell their own piss and shit and maybe learn how to keep they own houses."

If she had to wash and scrub, she'd save it for her own family, but only after her outdoor duties were done.

After rinsing and wringing out the last piece of clothing, she hangs her wash on the clothesline. She rushes inside her shack and eases down on a wooden rocking chair lined with cushions stuffed with handpicked cotton.

Mary reaches for a jar filled with olive oil, lemon juice, and sage sitting on the tea table next to her. She dips her fingers into the mixture and brings them to her hair, rubbing her scalp lightly, fractioning off patches, and twisting two strands together until they become one. She winds each twist around and around itself and tucks it at the root, creating a perfect knot. The finished product is like a fetus with its feet curled warmly against its head, and the beginning and end of its body joined seemingly forever. Mary wonders if that isn't the way it should be: if those months of safe incubation in one's own bodily fluids, tucked deeply into the self, is not the safest part of human existence, filled with a love that has no name and makes no claims.

She looks at her belly and smiles.

"I feel ya in there, baby boy," she says. "Me and your daddy can't wait to meet ya, but you's got a whiles to go." She hushes and cocks her head, waiting for a kick. She hears a rap on the front door instead. Wiping her palms on each side of her dress, Mary crosses the room. The heavy door groans under her pull.

"Mary." Burt's friend Handy stands on the bottom step, sweat moistening his nose even in the cool October air.

"Hiya, Handy. Step on inside." Mary waves him in and he follows. She leaves the door cracked and turns back to him. "Can I get you anything?" she asks, but then sees the sweat and the fear in Handy's eyes.

Her question shoots out sharply, "What ails you?"

Handy takes off his cap and holds it to his chest.

"I . . . I was at the store this morning. Some white men came for Burt. I didn't know what they wanted with him, but they let me go. I—"

"Where'd they take him? Where is he?"

"Well, see, that's what I'm trying to say to you, Mary." Handy wrings his cap. "I wanted to snoop around and see what it was they was up to . . . I did want to . . . but you never know, and I've got children to feed. I was too ashamed to come by earlier, and I was just praying, you know, that they was just there to give him a good talking to about his land and that they'd leave him be. But you and me know Burt, Mary. He might've flown off the handle."

"Handy," Mary's patience unravels, "just tell me the truth. Have you heard anything?"

"Well, now, see, that's what I'm tryna say to ya, Mary. I, myself, have not seen him, but my children—they wandered off a little while ago, like children do, you know, and they . . . they say there's a body hanging out in front of Piedmont Graveyard."

"Burt."

"The children saw the body from a distance and ran off," Handy says. "I didn't have my head on when I rushed over here. I shouldn't have . . ."

Blocks of yellow light fill Mary's vision, wavering and expanding. "I got to see," she murmurs.

"Mary, you really shouldn't." Handy reaches out to grab her, but the look in her eyes stops him cold. She runs down the steps, breezing past the hens scratching dirt between them as though they are playing a game. At the foot of a small hill, she turns right, her body picking up speed.

Mother Shelby, an elderly neighbor, hollers a startled cry to the back of Mary's bright-blue dress.

"What you tryna do, child . . . lose that baby?"

The black people's graveyard is just shy of a mile from Mary and Burt's house. Within minutes, Mary's heart is a beating knot in her chest, a thickening mass rising to choke her. Slowing, but not completely breaking her run, she raises her left hand and presses it hard against her right breast, where it feels like a large bone is snapping inside of her and on the verge of puncturing clear through her skin.

Mary slows to a walk when she spots the old white oak.

The tree stands at the rim of the graveyard, its squat and massive trunk holding muscular limbs offering tobacco-colored leaves.

Burt's body dangles from these limbs. He died facing the graveyard with the heavy knot of the noose pressing against the back of his neck.

Mary lets out a cry too deep for the length of her body, too old for the baby in her womb. The sound is dark and cold, and it ends as abruptly as it came, running back into the earth. Tears cling to Mary's eyelashes; they get stuck there, not falling. The strange, yellow, fractioned light inside them flickers to nothing.

Burt's body hangs low, low enough that Mary can touch his feet, his ankles, his calves. She walks around him, imagines the rope burning at his neck and unspoken words breaking down into letters in his throat, too high to go back down, forever trapped in the tissue and mucus there. She feels the tree branch shuddering as his weight is yanked against it; his neck snapping back, then forward; and his chin falling against his chest. It was his chin that had seemed so hard, so unyielding and so prideful, but Mary knew this was the very point of his tenderness and his weakness. Whenever she would take his chin into her mouth, the hardness and braveness would diminish in a quiver.

She circles him again and again as fallen acorns and twigs crack under her feet.

Everything is intact: his shirt and pants, his belt buckle, and even his shoes. The skin on his bald head is shiny and crease-less. His eyebrows are black and coarse and untamable. She had moistened her thumb this morning and smoothed them down, but they had curled back up as always.

"Wild, stubborn hair for a wild, stubborn man," she had playfully scolded him, lowering her eyes to his.

He had whispered back, "You would know."

And there is something else about Burt's person that Mary cannot see but feels: fright. She senses it and could cut it with a knife. But there is also the lingering spirit of regret and doubt and defeat about him. Those spirits hang around his body, stinking and drowning out the man she knew him to be. Mary feels, all of a sudden, ashamed, and she backs away, creating a gulf between herself and the oak, between Burt's body and hers. A sharp ache knocks her in the stomach, and the baby begins flipping in her womb like an acrobat, like a madman. And the bird on the branch over there near Burt—it won't stop chirp, chirp, chirping. And the sunlight, it keeps shining, casting a shaft that seems to set Mary's hair on fire. Yes, she is sure of it; she smells the smoke—feels it—and sees the great drops of sweat falling from her forehead, her scalp, her temples. She has to pee, feels her bowels threatening to let loose, and needs to throw up all at once. She folds over, but the morning's breakfast comes only as high as the bottom of her throat because she can't—she won't—let any of it go. Mary catches sight of Handy and what seems like the whole village of black townspeople running up behind her, and she takes it, all of it—the fetus, the piss, the puke, the shit—and compacts it, packs it all down into one tight constipated ball, and then stands up straight.

Handy lightly grabs Mary's arm. It is as slick as a seal.

"I'm so sorry, Mary. I'm so sorry. I'm so sorry."

The men come up behind Handy.

"We got to cut him down, Handy," one of them says, and the others nod.

Mary turns away. The women encircle her, moaning and rocking.

For a moment, Mary is tempted to lean into this rocking, to let their moans draw out her own, but she is not yet ready for this pity. For community. It suffocates her, and a wave of nausea returns. She looks over at the men, who are at the tree with Burt. They pray over his body and then pull out their pocketknives. Mary turns away once more, this time toward home.

She will not watch Burt coming down.

MARY STARES AT Old Sarge standing limply at the front door, his face the embodiment of sadness. Pastor Dan claimed dogs didn't have souls, but looking at Old Sarge's face, Mary wasn't so sure. Burt has been dead two months now, and Old Sarge hasn't broken his sad routine. She has no idea how to console him, how to tell him his beloved master would never return.

How the hell would she explain Burt's death to their son? A burst of anger spreads a column of heat around her neck, and for the first time since Burt was lynched, Mary's anger is clear and focused—not directed at some nebulous sea of whiteness. She had been avoiding going into town; she had not wanted to look at it, at the whiteness that murdered Burt. She did not trust her heart. Something in it wanted revenge.

But what is it whispering now?

Mary breathes in and out deeply, looking for the object standing at the end of this narrowing funnel of rage. She sees it finally: a familiar face. Burt's face lit by a slight smile.

Mary growls and gropes for the face, wanting to mar its perfect skin. But the face proves elusive, as not there as air. Mary pulls her hand back and watches this face that looks like Burt disappear. She curses his freedom, his big mouth, and his ego. Who the hell had he thought he was, fighting a white man? He had assured her that it was just a little scuffle, that all was okay, and that he and Winfrey's people had reached an agreement.

Lies. All of it. How many other lies had he told her?

Had he thought of her as he threw his own life away? Had he remembered they had a baby on the way?

She places her hand on her stomach. The baby has been so still lately—deadweight. But the heartburn she has been experiencing day and night reminds her that he is still very much alive and turning her guts inside out.

As she rubs her belly, Mary considers her own stillness. Since Burt's murder, she has not been able to finish anything, least of all her quilting. She can only do the work out there, under the open, unrestricted sky. It is work that is impersonal and bone exhausting but preferable to the small warm corners of her quilting chair—a place she used to love but now finds suffocating, a place of insufferable intimacy.

MARY'S DUE DATE is just a few weeks away. She lies sideways on the floor, feeling the baby curling inside her tighter and tighter. She closes her eyes and prays for the coiled mass of limbs to dissolve. She wishes it would stop feeding off her; she has no more to give it. She wishes it would shrivel to a seed and disintegrate into nothingness.

Nothingness has no temperature, no texture, no feeling. This nothingness holds itself just out of Mary's reach. Pain hides in every angle she turns.

Feeling helpless, Leola, who had looked after Mary after her mother died, sits near Mary, watching her.

"Child, don't you know? Your pain hopes you grow," Leola says after a while.

"I don't want to grow, Leola. All I want is to die."

Leola drops to the floor with a grunt and covers Mary's body with her own. "I know, child. I know. Come here."

In the older woman's forgiving arms, Mary's body loosens. Her tongue relaxes, and her words come in one smooth, coherent line.

"I'm so hard inside, and I don't think the hardness is ever gon' go away."

If only it would leave her numb, like a block of ice. That she could handle. But no, this hardness has sharp edges to it— edges that poke and prod.

"Mary, why don't you try listening to the hurt? I don't mean to make light of your pain, what you been through, but all I can tell you, hon, is to listen."

The baby is still, as though it is waiting to see if Mary can fulfill the task. Mary struggles to quiet the chaos in her mind. Thoughts tumble into her, one after the other, and she gets hung up on one: how she misses the smell of her own blood, that pungent smell that used to rise from her each month like clockwork; she is thirsty for its return. At least the menstrual cramps had been bearable, nothing compared to these days, where there is pain everywhere and no blood to show for it. Where is all the blood in the world? She cannot remember the last time she saw blood.

Burt's body had hung from that tree without a trace of blood on his skin or clothes. Blood is a witness.

Mary tries to imagine the baby growing inside her, full of blood that she cannot see.

Just a few months earlier, news of a lynched and mutilated pregnant black woman had traveled from Atlanta to Mississippi in all its bare horror. The woman had been seven months pregnant. A mob of men and women had pursued her with angry epithets and pocketknives. The knives grew warm and then hot in their hands. After men strung the woman to a tree, the knives inched curiously toward the woman's swollen belly, where life fought to hold on, even as its sustaining lifeline choked and strangled on its last few breaths.

The knives inched closer and closer still to the throbbing behind the cloth, behind the skin. First one knife and then another ripped away the woman's clothing. First one knife and then a dozen more tore through the skin. As urine and water gushed out, the fetus lay exposed, eyes still closed, and its body beautifully coiled.

The murderers and their accomplices fell silent in awe of the form and will of nature. The head of the mother's corpse fell forward, and so did the baby, with its twisted umbilical cord sliding to the ground like a snake unraveling from a tree, creating an S-like pattern in the dirt.

Mary shivers, remembering the whispers about the woman and her baby. What was the purpose of black life?

Even under Leola's care, Mary yearns for her own mother, to return to the days where she was in her mother's womb. She imagines unraveling her little curled fetal body and traveling back even farther than that: back to the day when she was just part of an egg, unconscious and free, and then even before that, back to the moment before she was even a figment of her mother's imagination.

Burt used to criticize her for what he called a "mighty funny way of looking at life."

"Look out the window," he would have told her.

Mary gets up and walks to the window. She sees a carefree sparrow perched on the thin limb of a plum tree.

"The world is not all bad, Mary," Burt liked to say. "The world is full of beauty and potential. Full of life and second chances."

Mary wipes her face. She looks at Leola, who is watching her with a worried frown. A small, bittersweet smile breaks Mary's dull countenance.

"Strange man, that daddy of his," she says, running the back of her hand over her stomach.

"He was that," Leola says. "And he would want you to go on, chile. I know that much about him."

With shame, Mary recalls the skepticism she would show Burt whenever he would tell her of his grandiose dreams and plans. Had she slowly snuffed the life out of him, causing him to settle for this godforsaken place?

"I got new ideas on things, Mary," Burt had said to her once. "We don't have to do what our mas and pas did—getting married young, dying in the same state of mind—or worse."

Mary had heard his plans before: He wanted her to finish learning how to read. He wanted her to spend less time trying to grow crops and join him in the store, which he regarded simply as a temporary vehicle that could get them out of Mississippi for good. He had his eye on California.

All of it had confused Mary to no end. On the one hand, he was as devoted to his store as she was to farming. He wanted to transform it from a little shack that sold dry goods, a smattering of produce, and odds and ends to a staple in the community where folks would gather and get freshly prepared food—her teacakes and fried chicken, for instance. He had even suggested changing the name Bridges Grocer to Mary's Teacakes & Groceries. It all sounded so warm and dandy the way he described it, and Mary had started baking batches of teacakes for the store every day but running a business like that with him full-time . . . she just didn't feel sophisticated enough to carry it out, and knowing that she would fall in love even harder for something he saw as just a means to an end—that had scared her.

She had looked at Burt and said, "Maybe what you're really saying is we're too good for our people here? Or you're too good."

The bitterness in her question had pressed against her pupils, sending pressure to the capillaries at the whites of her eyes. They had been eating supper, but Mary lost her appetite. She slid her plate of crowder peas and rice, ham hocks, collard greens, and cornbread away from her. She fiddled with a tear in the tablecloth.

"Don't you see, Mary? You're everything to me right now, just as you are. That's why I'm working so hard. You won't have to be all the time mending stuff like this tablecloth when we have the kind of life I want for us."

"Oh?" Mary said. "Rich folks' things don't rip?"

Burt laughed. "No, no—that's not it at all. See, they just hire somebody—somebody like you—to do all that kind of menial work for them, so they can focus on the big stuff. I want us to focus on the big stuff, Mary."

"You startin' to sound just like them white folk you say you can't stand."

Burt snorted.

"You just don't get it, Mary. Part of the reason I want to get our lives in order—and it ain't all about being rich—is 'cause I can't be one more man enslaving you. I watched my mama answering to the white man and my father, who treated her like his workhorse. I don't take kindly to folks saying you gotta do it this way; you gotta do it that way. I dig my heels in real hard."

"Why grow the store when what you really want is to hightail it outta here first chance you get?"

"Oh, Mary, don't you weep, girl," Burt said in a singsong tone. He winked, holding his hands out for her. "You still coming with me, aren't you?"

Mary swatted at his outstretched hands. "Oh, you gon' go whether I go or not?"

"Look," Burt said, trying again, "as bad as this place is for folk like us, I don't hate Mississippi, Mary, contrary to popular belief. I want to leave something here—this is my land; these are my people, the only people I know."

"Then why such a hot head to leave? Why not stay and care for the land, for these—your—people as you see them?"

"'Cause there's more to sowing and reaping than plantin' a bunch of seeds in the ground and waiting for 'em to die or sprout. And I'm not just gon' abandon the store. I have half a mind to deed it over to Handy. He been more like a brother to me than my own brothers, though I do get right annoyed with his knuckleheaded self some time. But he loves this place, and he ain't never going nowhere."

"And who'll take care of Handy's land while he up in your store tryna be you?"

"You seen all them children Handy got?"

Mary giggled, softening.

Burt seized the opening and moved his chair closer to hers. "He'll be fine," he said, lowering his voice, "and we gon' be fine, too, baby."

Mary shook her head, but not defiantly, more as though she were attempting to remove a few loose pieces of rice from a sack.

"I'm just spooked about big change is all," she said looking at Burt. "A lil' part of me gets all happy and excited about moving out to some new place. But a bigger part of me is downright frightened, Burt." She grabbed the sleeve of his shirt.

Burt ran his fingers over her tense ones.

"That ain't nothing special 'bout being scared," he said. "Hell, I got the chills, too, just hearing us sittin' here talk about it like this, and we at least another year off on making the move, depending on how well we can save and make plans."

"A year!"

"I said 'at least.' Mary, shaky as I am, I feel in my gut that California is the way for us."

Mary arched her brows. "The 'way'? I thought they say Jesus is the way. The way, the truth, and the light!"

"Yeah, and you know what? I think Jesus want us to follow him to California, woman."

"Shush up, man!" Mary said, pulling away from him. "You gon' get struck by lightnin'. But ain't it something, though?" she said, looking beyond Burt. "Might as well be another country, this California you all the time talkin' bout."

"Hell, I reckon it is like another country," Burt said and scooted his chair even closer to her. "They got all manner of strange flowers, even black flowers, out there. Desert. Ocean licking at the toes. They got great agriculture, too, and the oil . . . My cousin say they got these big old oil rigs that look like aliens landed right here on the earth. They stand in great big old fields drinking from the land. What they drinkin', baby, is better'n gold. It's black gold. It's power."

Mary would not be outdone. She motioned her head toward the window overlooking their small field. "Whenever I stand out there and turn the earth over with my hoe, and if it's black and soft, if I bend down and cup it up in my bare hands, and it's cool and thick and crumbles like cake . . . that feel like gold to me, baby," she said. "I dream of this field right here, growing as far as the eye can see. I dream of feeding dozens of people, not just us. I want us to own more of our own and use our own hands to create food for our people in Holmesville to enjoy. I been playing with some new recipes to expand on your teacakes idea. Making something right outta where you come from . . . like you are already doing . . . that to me is freedom, Burt. That to me is worth all the gold—or oil—in the world, as you say."

"I hear ya, Mary," Burt said. "But we ain't got no real rights here. We got this little piece of property. We got the store, and they want that too. I'm telling you, I can't live like this all my life. All's the time looking over my shoulder. Fighting to keep what us and our folks worked our skin down to bones to get. I'll kill one of 'em first."

Mary took in a sharp breath, looking at the walls as though they had ears.

"You ought not talk like that!"

Burt let out what felt like his and her breath combined and said, "I know, love. I know. But—"

"But? Always a 'but' with my Burt." Mary touched her fingertips to his chin. "Stop worrying and scheming so much, big fella. I need you here. We need you here. The young'uns look up to ya. They see what you done. How can we just abandon everybody like that, chasing after some dream so far away?"

Burt let out a long sigh, like a balloon finding its way back down to the earth. His shoulders dropped in acknowledgment. "You cut at the heart with that one 'cause I know you right," he said. "Lord knows I love everything we trying to do here, and I have high hopes for it." He stood, grabbed both of Mary's hands, and pulled her to her feet. He placed his hands on her hips and moved her in a slow dance to a melody only he could hear. His pupils darkened. "I love it when your fire meets my fire."

"What you talkin' 'bout?" Mary shook her head, laughing. "Why you changin' the subject?"

Burt laughed. "Naw, now, see, that's your mind in the gutter. I was talkin' 'bout yo passion, baby. You shoulda seen your eyes when you were talkin' about what you want to do here and the kids and everything . . . Shoot! That lit a fire under me all over again."

"Now, that's my man," Mary said, dragging the words out seductively.

Burt's hands moved to her backside. He squeezed.

"If you'll give me some of that sweet stuff, girl, hell, I might stay here forever."

In the recesses of Burt's mind, though, even as he had moved her toward the bed, he could hear a voice whisper, "Give it a year and see what happens. If things aren't going at the pace you'd like, bring it up again."

I can do that, he had thought, and he poured himself whole-heartedly into building the store, fixing up their little one-room home, and helping Mary extend her crops. They grew corn, tomatoes, okra, field peas, melons, greens, and squash.

"Never figured myself much of a farmer—that was Daddy's work, not mine—but you got some growing senses, woman," Burt had told Mary. "One thing's for sho: we ain't never gon' go hungry."

"Well," she had answered, "that was the idea all along."

"LEOLA," MARY SAYS, turning from her window, "what you know about California?"

"I know they got bright-orange poppies out there," Leola says. "I know it's better than here."

"Burt dreamed of moving us out there, but I thought he was crazy."

Leola walks over to Mary and drapes her arm around her shoulder. "Now the last thing I'm gon' allow you to do is beat up on my favorite girl. This here is all you know, chile. You had a right to be 'fraid. Don't close in on yourself now; it'll kill you. There's a great big ole world out there and Burt wanted y'all to see that. He still do. Heck, you could make a fortune selling your teacakes in any place."

"You saying I should leave? How on earth would you get on without me?" Mary gives Leola a wry smile.

"Hmph. Without you? You leave, I'm right on your tail."

LOSS OF LAND, LIFE, AND CAKE

IN JANUARY 2007, the fetus I was carrying was four months old. Each month, I consulted a website that used images and videos to help describe an unborn baby's typical development. I looked at the images of micro, translucent fetal limbs, curled bodies of otherworldliness, and worried about what was forming, or not forming, inside of me. I could not stop vomiting. Surely, I was depriving my baby of nutrition? But my doctor confirmed that the baby was growing fine, so I kept searching for remedies to curb my nausea and sweating spells. For the first time ever, I was grateful for the cooler days. My mood matched the drops in temperature and changing evening light, and I imagined us—earth, mother, baby—incubating together as one.

I would listen to Nina Simone sing "Another Spring" and think of Grandma Mary. I remembered how cold it used to get some Decembers and Januarys in DeRidder. As Nina sang, I remembered how the icicles would hang from our tin roof. I could see the frost covering the grass and bare fruit trees. I could hear the downpour of hail. I could feel the cold creeping through the gaping floorboards and into the house, taking a seat, and seeping into our bones. We'd stuff the cracks in walls and under doors with old rags and pray for the best. I'd hitch up my skirt and stand right over one of our gas heaters, willing fire into my marrow.

Then Nina's voice would turn a corner, skipping octaves, and I could smell the cut of fresh grass and honeysuckle, hear the birds, the flies, the bees, and Grandmama Avis's hums and chants. I could see Grandma Mary—back out on the porch, sipping sweet tea and thinking.

What, pray tell, was she thinking? Were her thoughts as obsessive as mine? A lifetime of pennies for her thoughts.

In my Los Angeles neighborhood, there is no Grandma Mary sitting on our front porch, no Miss Fannie Mae selling frozen cups and sugar cookies, no elders yelling from their front porches for kids to mind their manners, no Papa Houston or Uncle Cricket here to tell my child the stories they knew, and my heart will always ache with the knowledge of what my child will never know.

Grandma Mary's teacakes are not here; not a soul has the recipe. Mama does still have several of her old pots and pans. They have been used by four generations now. I remember cooking greens and peas (after shelling them on the front porch) in the big green cast-iron pot. And how much corn-bread had those pans held? I remember stirring slow-cooking meals with the serving spoon that has little holes that look like raindrops in it.

Grandma Mary cooked well into old age, and my mother says no one could figure out how or why her food was beyond extraordinary. Grandmama Avis was a consummate baker and cook but claimed she couldn't hold a candle to Mary. People around the world love soul food and Creole food; they attempt to replicate them, but authenticity, I think, has much to do with the actual burdens of living those lives. Those women had learned how to scrape together something delicious out of the fatback and pot liquor their oppressors did not want and how to make the stomach ache with want from a little flour and a little meal parceled out during the sting of the Great Depression.

Those old women didn't record or follow recipes; they threw food together, and that's how they taught us girls so that learning to cook was mostly through silent watchfulness, through osmosis and self-trust. Some call it magic, and black southern women take pride in the aura of mystery encircling their kitchens, in owning something that they pulled from deep within themselves and perfected until it brought a smile to their own lips. They take pride in the talent, creativity, and just plain scraping up of food and spice that is borne out of a need not only to feed but also to connect us to our origins, to nurture, to tell a story. Because Mary was a farmer, the food she cooked and served was planted by her hands. What we call "farm-to-table" now in fancy restaurantese. They were pioneers of this ground-to-mouth magic—passed on, no doubt, by our ancestors whose whispers Mary must have remembered long after leaving Mississippi, whose flavors she enhanced and used as inspiration to create her own. Mary took hold of whatever parcels of land she could; she communed with it; she gathered the harvest it blessed her with; she used it to show us a part of who she was—a part that could not be stolen or denied.

Still.

I wish at least one of us had gained and retained the secret of her biscuits, of her teacakes.

Death, distance, and ambition have erased all of those things from my life. Until my pregnancy, the absence of these things had not preoccupied my mind, but how could I tell my child that this—this little patch of property in Los Angeles is all I have to pass on? Even the house on Elm has now been torn down. The fruit trees are all gone. My mother still owns the property, but she has long lived in Florida, and health problems prevent her from traveling often. Our land on Elm street sits forlorn.

Mary's farmland, all of it, is gone too—squandered: lost to

overgrowth, unpaid taxes, and bad management by an uncle. On the surface, it appears that none of us has cared much about our legacy until some fixation overcomes one of us. My sister Dena, for instance, became obsessed with duplicating Grandma Mary's teacakes by using her taste-bud memory and recipes she found online.

She emailed me a recipe called "Old Fashioned Southern Tea Cakes" by a woman named Pearline that called for sifted plain flour, salt, baking powder, butter, sugar, eggs, vanilla, and milk. It sounded so simple. Whenever Uncle Junior would preach about God raining down manna on the Israelites, I would sit on the pew and let my mouth water. Surely, Grandma Mary's tea cakes were manna. Surely, there was some godly secret ingredient that Pearline could not know.

"I always remembered that first bite from Grandma's tea cakes," Dena wrote. "Barely tall enough to tiptoe and look over a table, I recall being anxious to taste them.

"I used this recipe as a guideline but remembered tasting some spices and added some allspice and a little nutmeg. That made a huge difference. Can't remember exactly how much and if I used lemon or vanilla extract. I think I used lemon. And I tried to shape them like Grandma did."

In the photos she sent me, her cakes resembled sugar cookies, wide and flat and a bit pale. I had no doubt they were delicious, but my excitement over the possibility that she had somehow re-created our Mary's tea cakes, thereby providing us with an heirloom that we and our children could eat, re-create, and pass on, fell flat.

IN MY BACKYARD are blackberry vines, cherry tomatoes that grow like wildfire, and a mature guava tree—broad-shouldered and tall. I love to see the first buds of the guava sprouting, to smell the floral scent of the guavas—a scent of rosewater, earth, and honey—and to watch when they ripen and fall to the ground. The problem is that this process does not happen every year, the gardener tells me. It often skips a year. In the years that the tree does not produce, it is easy to dismiss it, to see it as just another tree, to forget what kind of tree it is. Genealogy is like that. Certain traits and obsessions can skip a generation, or two, before settling on a new embryo like pollen.

In addition to scrolling websites, I read books about what was going on inside my body as the embryo took on a more definite shape and prepared to feed on me in increasing quantities, to reposition my internal organs, to overhaul my hormones, and to refine my mental capacities. Having all of this digital information, complete with diagrams and videos, at my fingertips made me think of Grandma Mary carrying a baby inside of her for the first time with death fresh and heavy on her shoulders. It doesn't seem right: to simultaneously hold in your imagination the skull of your dead lover and the soft developing skull of his baby.

Houston was the only child she birthed. She bore no children for John Buckley, although she stayed married to him until he died of old age. Houston carried her and Burt's line, carried within him proof of her and Burt's love. He grew into a man who fathered nine children, including my mother, seven sons and the daughter outside of his marriage. Grandmama Avis left him for his philandering, but she returned eventually, and they were together until death parted them again.

The fate of their children's marriages followed theirs— troubled, twisted with infidelity, abuse, and, in at least one case, incest. All of their children's first marriages ended in divorce, sometimes with second and third marriages following suit.

Papa Houston and every last one of his sons were hard men, broad in spirit and shoulder—men used to labor. Even the physically small ones, Uncle Cricket and Uncle David, had an air of bigness about them. Following in their father's footsteps, several of them made their livelihoods in the lumber business, sawing and chopping down trees with a vengeance and burying sticks of dynamite in the ground to blow up the thick roots. The way they worked, the way they refused to retire from the woods even when it was time for them to give it up, it was as though something was after them, riding the muscles in their backs as they hacked away.

What is the relationship between the two—a love cut short by racial violence and the generational trail of broken people in its wake? Could Marcus and I, two people with nothing substantial to hold on to but the fading wispiness of romantic fantasies, create a better legacy?

There are tales of an uncle beating his wife and children, of another sexually molesting his daughters. And when Dena and I were girls, one of those uncle's sons crept into our house in the dead of night and tried to lure Dena outside. In hand, he had a rope, a handkerchief, and some kind of liquid to, we presumed, knock her unconscious. Fortunately, even in her grogginess, Dena realized that he was up to no good and yelled for help, and the boy went running back into the night. Today, he spends time in and out of jail as a convicted sex offender.

Are the men in my family cursed? What made some of them want to harm, or to consume, their own flesh? I believe there is a crime bigger than each individual offense, that we never got to the root of our original sickness: who the first family was, what was done to them, and how Mary chose to suppress it preprogrammed us. She is not fully to blame. The coding—slavery, subsequent generations of trauma—was already set.

I am no better than my blood. All I have tried to do is decipher the equation so that I can keep what worked well for us and disconnect that which caused us to malfunction as a family, as people.

I MOVED TO California with thirty years of Louisiana in my blood—thirty years of its heat, its sheer heat, and the hairy mosquitoes that rise from swamp water to needle my skin with a steady intravenous drip of venom. I am at one with that climate's oppressiveness: my bones need marrow-deep heat; my skin expects humidity as thick as velvet. I have skin designed to take in the sun and hold it forever.

When we are from the country, when we are from down there, we carry star-studded black skies with us to cities whose skies are polluted by artificial light. We bring the creaking of floorboards, the *thwack* of splitting wood, the circus surround sound of cicadas and crickets. We bring unmarked graves decorated with plastic flowers the color of the candy necklaces we used to eat from around our moist necks. We bring the taste of our own skin's salt into our mouths and of just-slaughtered pigs, the gamey toughness of cooked coon and rabbit, the pop of BB guns. We bring the unsolved mysteries that live in the woods and in our own homes, the memory of our father's, papa's, uncle's, grandma's rifles. Gun control? We will remember that this means something else entirely to the black southern family.

Physically, I left it all behind, but the South comes to me, over and over, in broken memories, in fleeting dreams and visions, especially when I am at my weakest, plagued by chronic fatigue, which doubled in power during my pregnancy. I am convinced this vague sickness is the residual venom of the creatures of my native land. The fatigue, which blankets me without warning, causes me to fear the hidden parts of my body, and within that fear stands vulnerability, an open door through which the dead glide, offering items that, on the surface, seem nice but upon closer inspection are anything but real: an exquisitely designed teapot filled with plastic, garish flowers, for instance. In my dreams, the gift bearer is always someone I knew—someone I loved. Their presence stirs within me both a desire to cling and to avert.

But I have always allowed particles from other people's souls to dart past the physical boundary that is my body. More accurately, I never learned how to prevent these infiltrations; I believed I had no choice. Shards of alien souls float around inside me, lost in my galaxy, and end up—always—colliding with my intestinal bodies, something substantial yet penetrable. They set up lodging there, trying to take root and integrate as family, but my brain sends signals of rejection and alarm, producing acute cramps that meld into a constant churning of dull and chronic ache. Sometimes, I hear those foreign pieces of soul sniffling, searching for their origins, dripping wet sound into my bloodstream until it reaches my inner ear.

"If a dead person ever offers you something, don't take it," some of my relatives, when they were living, used to warn. When they visit my dreams, I try to show them my love, to offer them what I have: A bucket of fresh flowers in water. Something from the land of the living.

"See," I told an image of Papa Houston once, "these are real flowers." I thrust the flowers at him, but he would not accept them. I got the sinking feeling that he could see inside me and did not like what was there: distrust.

Years ago, it was true: I did not want something I could not touch peering into me, did not want the breath of the dead on my skin. But now I open myself to these things. I stand inside an open window welcoming the strong Southern California flushes, each sensation a word skating across my arms.

MARY, 1904

WHAT IF THE world has already ended, and we just don't know it yet?

Mary wakes with a start. The question whispers from the inside of her waking consciousness and lodges there. The morning is too quiet. Where are the birds? She runs to the front door and swings it open. She takes a deep breath and then lets it out.

"How can this not be real? The world has not ended," she says aloud and then remembers her pain: Burt is gone.

She feels the familiar empty thud in her chest but is for the moment more unsettled by the waking question. It scares her. It makes her feel alive.

Standing there on the threshold as the cool, moist November air lets her know that she is, indeed, still alive, that the world is still very much alive, Mary's water breaks.

PART II

WEIGHT OF CHILDREN

"I ALWAYS SAID I wanted five children, but I didn't want y'all like this."

Mama was sitting up in her bed as she spoke, mostly to herself. Her white polyester slip was raised over her round belly. She sat cross-legged in the middle of the bed with bills spread around her as she punched buttons on her calculator's keypad with her long brown index finger. I was sitting at the foot of her bed.

"I come from a big family, so I wanted a big family," she continued. "But I pictured it with a husband and my own house and happy kids. Not like this. With bills I can't ever pay. Men who don't want to be the daddies they are. Kids I can't buy for."

It was 1984. I was thirteen, Dena was going on twelve, and Michie was five. Mama was thirty-one, and pregnant again.

The first man Mama had warmed up to after leaving my father was a soldier. She and Charles were friends, but they were not in love. When she got pregnant with Michie, she was still in her twenties and was not ready for remarriage. By her early thirties, she was lonely and ready to settle down, and she had returned to believing love could happen the way it did in her Harlequin romance novels—initial conflict, sure, but after that becoming something sweet and rapturous and everlasting.

When Mama met Roan, she was sure he was her knight. He

was dark, handsome, and full of well-trained muscle. We girls fell in love with him too.

But Roan wasn't ready to be a father. Mama turned her head in my direction without focusing on my face. "I hope you girls never have to go through what I've been through."

I thought my heart would just about burst when she told me how Roan had left her.

Their courtship had ended just outside our house, where the plums were still bright green, grass-snake green, the way I like them: tart and hard and begging for salt, an astringent against the teeth.

Roan had driven from Fort Polk, the military base just north of DeRidder, after Mama had told him she desperately needed to see him.

She was already outdoors when he pulled up. Roan stayed on his motorbike with his hands tight on the bars. I imagined Mama walking over to him with her head down and arms dangling at her sides.

"I'm pregnant, Roan."

Spite, pure and immediate, laced Roan's words.

"How do I know it's mine?"

The streetlight buzzed, growing louder and sharper—a crackling protest of electricity, a swarm of insects descending.

"Now, come on, Roan. You know I haven't been with anyone else."

"Well, you're gonna need to get an abortion."

The salt was on Mama's tongue before she knew she was crying.

"I'll never kill any baby of mine."

"I don't want it, Pam. I'm being transferred anyway, so I've been thinking . . ."

The rest of his speech was lost on her as she marveled at how her body continued to stand while inside it swooned with a dizzying sickness. Roan used her shocked silence to his advantage. She watched his rigid back on the gleaming motorcycle as he zoomed off into the night.

The army transferred Roan to Hawaii, and we never saw him again. He sent Mama's letters—her pleas, her love, her anger—back to her unopened.

Mama had what family members called a nervous breakdown that fall. It started in her mouth and set her nerves on edge. Doctors couldn't find the source of the pain. She took a leave of absence and closed herself up in her room. The slightest noise grated on her, and she squealed out in pain and frustration for us kids to shut up.

Dena and I tiptoed around her. We cleaned. We cooked. We helped Grandmama take care of Michie.

To offset her lost salary, Mama had to sign up for welfare temporarily. She despised being on welfare and would later remind us that she was only on it for a few months. I stayed constipated from eating so much government-issued food, especially the heavy bricks of processed cheese. We made cheese sandwiches, cheese toast, and melted cheese to pour over spaghetti. I refused to drink the government's version of calcium: chunks of powder that were supposed to turn water to milk. After Dena and I shelled field, black-eyed, and purple-hull peas on the front porch, we followed Grandmama Avis's instructions on cooking peas with ham hocks. We washed, cut, and cooked collards, turnips, and mustard greens. We cut up whole chickens and whole onions and smothered them with seasonings and flour in Grandma Mary's old cast-iron skillet. In the evenings, we brought steaming plates of white rice, peas, chicken, and greens to Mama's bed. The evenings could get away from you when they were filled with chores. If someone inquired about the status of our homework, I can't recall, although the expectation that we do well in school was clear.

That April, Mama had a son. She named him Nicholas, and we fawned over him because he was the only other male in the house besides Papa.

"Hey, little Nick-Nick," we sang to him, gazing at his long eyelashes and smooth yellow-brown skin. I thought of his father often: When was Mama going to do something about Roan? Make him pay?

The love I once had for Roan, the adoration, made my hunger for revenge that much stronger. I fantasized about the day he'd show up, begging to see his son. I would stand firmly in the doorway and look him dead in the eye.

"Look how tall you're getting," he would say with a nervous smile spreading his lips.

I would keep staring at him with my coal-black eyes until his feet shifted and his tongue twisted on itself.

"You are not welcome here," I would say, finally. "You are not welcome here, you bastard. Yes, you are the bastard—not my baby brother."

I practiced how I would say bastard over and over again. I wanted to deliver it to Roan like it was the nastiest thing that had ever been in my mouth.

But he never came.

And meanwhile, some relatives talked about Mama like she was a dog. With the first pregnancy after her divorce, they had felt sorry for her, but after the second time, and with no new husband in sight, judgment filled their eyes.

"How she gon' have all them kids in your house like that, Mama?" Uncle Herbert asked.

"Folks around town talkin' 'bout her real bad. Real bad," Uncle Billy Joe told Grandmama Avis.

"And what you say, Billy Joe, huh, when they drag your sister's name through the mud?" Grandmama asked. "Do you just stand there like your tongue's been cut out your mouth? Do you take up for her? Or do you join in on the name-calling?"

He hung his head.

Uncle Boo, the quiet one, stared at his youngest brother and curled his lip. I looked down at the black oil spotting up Uncle Boo's T-shirt, which had long ago forgotten it was white. He'd been working on one of the trucks he kept out back in my grandparents' yard. His trucks were an eyesore, and he and Mama had gotten into it a few times over him turning our yard into a junkyard. But out of all the brothers, Boo would be the one to snatch somebody up if he caught them talking about his baby sister. To him—and to Uncle Cricket—she was still an innocent little thing running around, gullible to the wiles of the world. A world they had long ago learned not to trust.

But Mama's nature was to trust. She'd been born when her parents were at the end of their prime. And as she grew up in the midfifties to late sixties, despite the state of the world for black folks, things just weren't as hard at home for her parents as they had been when her brothers were growing up. She was surrounded by blankets of love and protection. Papa spoiled her rotten, and her brothers, some of them old enough to be her daddy, weren't much better. Why would she believe that men were not to be trusted? That they would not scoop her up and sail away with her the way it happened for those white ladies in her novels?

She thought her daddy was the world until she found out he'd fathered another child outside of his marriage.

"Mama, how could Daddy have done that to you?" she would ask her mother, her dark eyes spitting black sparks.

"Oh, PamaJean, that was long ago, honey. That's old water under a bridge."

"But why'd you stay with him, Mama?" she asked. "How could you? And how did you take his daughter in like that, like she was your own?"

Grandmama told her that she didn't expect her to understand the first thing about love or marriage or what kind of mind full of holes and lust and pain her daddy had to fight against even after he turned his life around. She didn't try to explain to her, at the time, how she had left Papa for a while and gotten into a relationship with another man before coming back to give her and Houston another try. Perhaps she hated him, but she still loved him. He had grown up fatherless, and her mother had died when she was eleven. Neither of them wanted their children to suffer those same voids.

"The Bible says love covers a multitude of sins," Grandmama liked to say. She could've gone around rubbing Papa's face in his manure all day long if she wanted to, but she didn't have to because it took him the rest of his life to forgive himself for all his transgressions.

THREE YEARS AFTER my brother Nick was born, Mama was pregnant again, fulfilling her childhood wish to have five children. No, she hadn't wanted us like that—single and broke and living in her parents' house—but there we were anyway.

"I've been somebody's mama for so long," she said, "I don't know what it's like to be a teenager. I didn't get to enjoy those years."

And now, I thought, she was taking mine. As the eldest, I already felt like a mama, a secondhand mama. When Mama got pregnant the fifth time, I turned on her.

I turned on her when she needed me most.

"I have something to tell you, Sand," she said after calling me to her room one evening. She was standing near the foot of her bed, still wearing her work clothes—an A-line skirt and button-down blouse.

"I know you have a lot on you already, so I didn't know how to tell you, but I'm going to have another baby. Everybody knows. I just didn't know how to tell you."

I don't know if I was angrier about the pregnancy or that

she had made me the outsider by withholding information that everyone else knew. I wanted to be the instigator of my outsider status, not have it assigned to me.

I looked down at her spreading hips and then left the room.

I was determined to separate myself from her. My life was going in a different direction than the one her choices were paving for me. I had plans. I had a boyfriend I didn't want to marry until we had finished college and started our careers. I had friends whose parents were middle class, whose mothers didn't have young children, whose parents didn't presume, as far as I knew, that when their phones rang it was an irate bill collector. I ran to their nicely decorated homes for refuge.

Mostly, I ran to my best friend Melanie S.'s house. Her mother, Marie, shook her head when I told her Mama was pregnant again. Marie only had one child. She was stylish and pretty and petite, with thick hair framing her perpetually made-up caramel face and eyelids shaded in jewel tones.

Her stomach was flat, the rest of her curvy. I could recall a time when Mama's stomach was flat, when she used to do upside-down bicycle exercises on the floor in her bedroom, crunching her knees into her abdomen. She was never as curvy as Marie, but her hips used to span out from her small waist like a pleated hand fan.

"Hasn't your mom ever heard of the word *condom*?" Marie asked.

"Well, she said it was a mistake. She said that Fred tricked her."

"Isn't she a little too old to be getting tricked?"

"Too old to be having more babies, that's for sure," I mumbled.

Marie's laugh was more of a snort. "Those churchgoing women kill me. Always talking against birth control and for-nication but always winding up with swollen bellies. I mean, you all are already struggling. What on earth is she going to do now?"

"I don't know, Miss Marie. Can I move in with you and Melanie? I don't feel like taking care of her children anymore."

"You can stay whenever you like," Melanie said and hugged me.

But Mama caught on to me real quick. It was my turn to bathe Nick one night. I had worked several hours at my after-school job as a grocery store clerk at the Piggly Wiggly across town. I had cooked, and I had cleaned while my homework sat in a corner—notes for a test untouched. Mama walked into the kitchen. Sourness sagged her face.

"Can I go home with Melanie after school tomorrow?" I asked.

"No," she snapped.

"Why not?"

She walked up to me, and I backed up a little, the refrigerator at my back.

"You always wanting to spend the night over there," she said. "This is your home. You've got plenty of work to do here. You act like you can't stand to be inside your own house. What is so great about Melanie and Miss Marie?"

I stared boldly, directly, into her eyes. What was it she saw in my eyes? Disdain? A challenge? Disgust? Whatever it was, it must have unnerved her. She slapped me across the face. The back of my head hit the refrigerator with a thud.

"You don't talk back with your mouth, but you talk back anyway, don't you, Miss Sand? It's all in your face. A person can just glance at your face and see what's in your heart."

My cheek burned, and the back of my head held a dull ache, but I refused to cry.

"Go on and give your little brother his bath. Somebody had to wash your dirty behind when you were a little kid too. Somebody had to take care of you."

But I didn't ask to be born, I wanted to scream. And I didn't have these children.

Another thought came to me, crawling across my consciousness like a turtle crossing a quiet dirt road: I'm never having children.

It thrust itself deep inside me, filling me completely. And I welcomed it. Nurtured it. I was sixteen when it made its first sound, a mumble still caged behind my teeth. By my seventeenth birthday, it had gained all the iron it needed. *Never*, I silently swore, and girls everywhere must have joined my heart's declaration. A million cords tightened within my chest. My mind sealed itself.

Never.

I imagined Mama's face twisting and crumbling with pain and disbelief. She would regard my stance as the ultimate strike against her. She would interpret it as my final foray into a life that had nothing to do with hers.

I didn't care. She could yell and slap my face again. But I would keep saying it over and over with wild laughter erupting from my mouth and my eyes.

Never. Never. Never.

MARY, 1903

MARY KNOWS THAT the only way to hold on to a scent is to fold it into the crevices of your skin. First, you have to treat the skin from the inside out. Leola once taught her how to emit oil from flowers to pull out their deepest essences. She taught her how to pluck the best flower from a bush, how to run her finger over its moist petals, and how to separate them from each other before reuniting them in a jar of pre-poured oil.

Mary places her finger in the jar and watches the flower pieces roll into the tunnel her finger creates. She closes the jar with a lid and places it on a shelf to marinate for two weeks. The petals float. The oil listens.

When the flower oil is ready, Mary readies her bath. She opens the jar, and the oil, having become one with the flower, springs forth its perfume. Mary sips a quarter of it. The scent will seep out of her pores later. She pours a small cup of it in her palm, inhales, and then lets it fall from her hand into the tin washtub of water. She slips her body into the tub and opens her legs. She is thinking of Burt. This evening, she will meet him down by the river. They are not married yet, but Mary makes up her mind right then and there, sitting in the tub, that tonight will be their first time. She will not wait. They will not wait to become flower and oil merged.

They are at the river. Burt's body is over Mary's body. He

smells like grass, and he smells like the earth: sweet, dark. Mary has tasted dirt and grass before, and so he tastes familiar. She is over him now. He places his hands on her hips, not to steer but to hold on, and he wonders at the wild smell of her. It flows from her elbows, her neck, the roots of her hair, and all the places he cannot see.

Mary knows it is better to give flowers to the living.

The river grows black and still, swallowing the sound of every living thing: the cacophony of crickets, the whisper of water over moss, the moaning of man and woman.

In a little while, the world will come for them: the white men with their guns and their pitchfork hearts, the law with its blind eye, will come for them.

But for now, all of those threats are held at bay as this black woman and this black man make love, make life, with the river and the trees and the night covering them.

SEED OF STRANGE FRUIT

OCTOBER 22, 2006

Nausea. Constant nausea. This stark ache rising in my belly . . . what I wonder is if the baby feels it, swimming in this wave of nausea. I have not vomited yet, only felt like it. I pray this goes away. The fatigue is manageable—I can eat better, get more rest, work out less. But this—this constant motion sickness—is unbearable.

I want the baby. I just want to feel good while I am carrying it.

MEMORY IS A woman. Subtle, haunting, devastating. Right even when she is wrong.

If Grandma Mary were still alive, would she be able to describe in detail what her pregnancy was like? Who was around to hold her anger and pain for her? I suppose that is what I am trying to do, to swaddle her old pain like a little baby, to rock it back and forth, back and forth, until I can no longer hear its cries, and I can lay it down to rest in peace.

My generation—my siblings and first cousins—is two generations removed from Mary and Burt; still, we carry a percentage of them both inside of us. My cousins and Dena continued that lineage long before I decided to join the ranks. Dena had a son when she was nineteen (the age our mother was when she had Dena), and there are cousins younger than I who have multiple children. I think of their offspring as Mary and Burt's harvest, as they were their ancestors' harvest. Mary loved the land, planting and tilling and producing. We are her crop. A latecomer, I was humbled to oversee another season.

But there were days where I doubted I could go through it.

Before pregnancy, each month I expanded into a swollen pocket of water and blood and ache. Pain encircled my abdomen and moved down to my hips and the insides of my thighs. Even my buttocks would ache. I didn't miss those monthly meetings, didn't miss the pungent scent of my own blood, but I didn't love pregnancy either.

Some women adore pregnancy. They bask in renewed energy. Their skin glows; their hair glistens. Their eye sockets and teeth sparkle a new white.

This was not my experience. I stayed sick. Once the morning sickness finally abated, severe heartburn struck my esophagus. My doctor diagnosed it as gestational heartburn, but I have never known heartburn like that—like a mountain of wild boars clamoring inside my chest and scratching a path up my throat. It made me gag and vomit violently. I vomited all over Los Angeles and its periphery—on the sides of freeways and streets. At the base of a stop sign in a neighborhood not my own. At a fancy Italian restaurant and at the beach.

What is this child *doing* on the inside of me? I wondered. I consulted the web to recall the order of the body's building blocks: first atom, then molecules, cells, tissues, organs. The skeletal system is the axis, giving shape and form to this mysterious galaxy of gelatinous objects. Revisiting grade-school biology, I tried to take on an appreciation of the body forming inside of mine, but my threshold for pain and sickness is low.

As a cherry on top of the nausea, I developed a rare skin disorder that only pregnant women get and just 1 percent of pregnant women: pruritic urticarial papules and plaques of pregnancy, or PUPPP. It started at my navel and spread up my belly, my chest, and then over my shoulders and down my back. The itch felt like a thousand stinging ants crawling just underneath the dermis.

I am allergic to this baby, I thought. I read that the disorder strikes mothers carrying male fetuses, and thought, No, no, no—can't be. I can't be carrying a boy.

Marcus and I believed we would have a little girl. I could almost feel it. I could almost see her. I would be able to help her build the confidence she would need from an early age—the confidence that I didn't have. And since Marcus already had two sons, he wanted to father a daughter. I would love to see up close that kind of father-daughtering that is absolutely foreign to me. I wanted—needed—to see him spoil her. We talked about our dreams for her. We believed that a black girl given the love and attention she needed early would have a better chance to thrive. In addition to the statistics, we could point to ourselves as evidence. Even with the absence of a supportive father and growing up poor, I had found a way to go to college and string together a career while Marcus had been detoured from the college path he thought he was on through, first, an older neighbor persuading him to take his first hit of crack, and, second, the allure of the streets. A fear that his sons might fall prey to a similar cycle was a fear that linked him and his ex-wife inextricably.

When I think about the childhoods Marcus and I had, as well as our early adult lives, I see two people swimming upstream in a river of stereotypes, willing the loud rush of our proclaimed love for each other to drown out the improbability of our survival. To outsiders and even somewhere just underneath the top layers of desire and optimism within us burned the whispered question: *How on earth will this relationship work?*

We were bruised, and we had bruised. But to the casual observer, we looked shiny and whole. Together, in the California sun, we were striking—golden brown and glowing like pieces of fruit hanging from a tree. But imagine the underside of seemingly perfect fruit, the underside hiding from eyes and the sun, half-eaten by wasteful birds, by bacteria, and by time. Obstinate, determined to prove some point, it refuses to fall to its complete death. Or maybe it is the branch that hangs onto the fruit, maybe it is the branch that won't let the fruit go.

In its youth, the fruit had been firm with promise; neither time nor birds bear the brunt of its demise. Not fully. The soil the tree was planted in was already contaminated, and contaminated soil cannot produce pure fruit. Rot rises in its roots, climbs up its trunk and into its limbs, leaves, and seeds, which become the fruit.

Call us strange, but we, like so many others before us and so perhaps not so strange, hoped against hope. I knew there were real-life healthy black families. Why couldn't we become one of them? Our families' brokenness predated them. So much of it was out of their control. America had been pecking at them far longer than the existence of the family members we could point to and say, "This is who so-and-so was. This is their story. This is why they were the way they were. This is who begat them. This is what they left their children and what their children left their children."

Men can pass down stories. Men are griots, but the woman's body holds a universe of bodies and, therefore, stories. Memory is a woman, and Mary's body held a universe of memories. She held that universe away from us in many ways, and yet my pregnant body connected me to her.

"At least you know who your great-grandparents were," Marcus said once. "I know my grandmother on my mother's mother's side, but not on her father's side and have no idea who my dad's parents and grandparents were. I believe they were from Louisiana, but I'm not sure."

JUST AS MY mother had given birth to me at seventeen, Marcus's mother had given birth to him, her first child, when she was seventeen. Like my mother, she had bad turns with men over the years, the most traumatic with a physically and emotionally abusive man who was a heroin addict. As a boy, Marcus had watched this man shoot needles into his arm and then nod from his drug-induced otherworld. He watched him become animated with rage, too, when he was not high. He beat Marcus, beat his mother, and sent Marcus to the corner store to buy booze and cigarettes. The setting was early 1980s South Central Los Angeles. Who would be surprised by what drew young Marcus in—gang life, petty thefts, fights at school, which resulted in suspensions and time in juvie?

"You guys must have moved a thousand times," I tell him as we drive around Los Angeles. He is always pointing to some apartment building he used to live in ("There's the one my brother burned down") or some school he attended for a year or half a year.

Marcus didn't meet his own father until he was fourteen. He was on a bus with his mother when he saw a man staring at them intently. The way the man was staring, and something about the structure of his face, unsettled Marcus. He turned to his mom and saw how tense she was.

He leaned in and whispered, "Mom, is that him? Is that my dad?"

"Yes," she affirmed.

Marcus, his height belying his age, ambled to the back of the bus without spite, only a curious hunger.

"Are you my dad?" he asked the man, and his father did not deny him. It was Marcus, though, who pursued the relationship that, over the years, proved disappointing.

Still, every year or so, he'll try to get his father to take an interest, if not in him, then in one of his grandsons.

Four years after Marcus was born, my mother married my father in 1970, delivering me a year later and Dena a year and a half after my birth. That marriage, wrecked by my father's emotional, financial, and physical abuse, ended after seven years, and I watched my mother broken by one relationship after another, bringing three more children into this world. Somehow, romance and childbearing got all tangled up in my head, and I decided I would take the romance but not the baggage. The way I figured it was that if a man messed up on me, I could leave free and clear. I didn't realize that the same tendency for messing up was lying dormant inside of me.

I TOLD MARCUS about a dream I had of a little girl when I was still with my ex-husband. In the dream, the little girl was driving a long, old car, maybe a Cadillac, although she could barely see over the steering wheel.

In the dream, Ric and I were running on a sidewalk—not for exercise; there was fear in us, as though something was chasing us; we were running for our lives. The little girl pulled the car up to the sidewalk with a screech.

"Get in," she said, and we got in.

I reached out my hand to touch her little face, but then I woke up. "I had such a strange dream," I said to Ric minutes after waking, but as I described it to him, I could feel him closing up. He would not let me pull him down the hole of interpretation and what-ifs. He wanted to be the only one steering his ship.

"Hmm," he said as he hung fresh laundry in the closet. "Not sure what that means."

"I want to know who she was, Ric," I pressed. "She seemed so familiar, like someone I've met or have to meet."

For months, I journaled about the dream and my decision not to have children. I also wanted to find a way to build a closer relationship with my mother. I wrote and said that I regretted the pain that had separated us for years and that I did not want to live the rest of my life feeling resentful. I did not want to make life decisions based on my childhood.

"What would be so bad about us having a child?" I mustered up the courage to ask this of Ric.

He was, as I expected he would be, taken aback.

"Wow, really? I thought we had decided on this, Sand."

"We did. I'm just feeling these weird tugs in my body . . . and in my mind. I don't know what is going on with me. Maybe it's teaching the kids. They're big kids, but so many of them are hurting. Their stories are so sad."

But Ric was not interested in trying to right the wrongs of bad parenting by having our own child. He did not trust himself to do that. We both had agreed that we would not take a chance at trying to rear a healthy child in a world that was still so crazy. Not when we had not had the best of childhoods. Not when we were absorbed in pursuing our own dreams.

"One thing I've noticed about people who have children is that they envy those of us who don't, those of us who have our freedom," Ric had said once.

I linked my teaching experiences to my budding change of heart. But in Ric's eyes, I didn't get to change my mind in the middle of our marriage. Besides, how much of my yearning was biological and how much had erupted from an internal sense of emptiness, or worse—an ancient well that could never be filled?

MARY, 1904

MARY HASN'T HAD her baby in her arms for long before her visiting aunt, Verna Bell, and Verna Bell's church sisters start fussing over her future, their voices like the scratching fingernails of a child infected with chicken pox. The women peel back the newly formed scabs of Mary's hurt and poke.

"What you gon' do, Mary, now that that young man of yours is gone?" Mary's aunt Verna Bell asks. Verna Bell and her husband live down the road from Mary, but Leola feels far more like family than the two of them.

"I'm gon' be fine, Aunt Verna," Mary says.

A woman named Hattie Mae jumps in. "Sister Verna is right. You gon' need a man for that baby. A daddy."

"He has a daddy," Mary says.

"*Had* a daddy," Hattie Mae shoots back.

Mary doesn't like the woman's tone, how it makes her feel as if she is the one responsible for shortchanging her baby, for depriving him of something he desperately needs.

"The fact that they killed his daddy don't change the fact that Burt is his daddy," she says. She waits a beat. "Burt was gon' get us outta here. It's this place and all the people in it that's the problem."

Hattie Mae shakes her head. "Is that right?"

"Yes, ma'am, it sure is. And I shoulda listened to him earlier. He'd still be alive."

Hattie Mae grunts. "That boy'd still be alive if he wouldn've had such a hot head."

Angry tears well in Mary's eyes, but before she can form a retort, Leola clears her throat from her corner of the room where she has sat quietly knitting a blanket for the baby.

"Alrighty now, let's leave the gal be."

"All we saying is, you can't take care of this baby by yo'self." There is a hint of disdain in Verna Bell's voice, and Mary thinks of the story of Job and his so-called friends and all their naysaying.

She laughs, a biting sound designed to insult. "Auntie, women been doing it for thousands of years."

"Yeah, but with lots of help. Your mama gone. Your daddy following every strip of railroad work he can find. You and Burt was over here living in your own little world, trapped in your own heads, but you gon' need help now. And while's Leola done always had a soft spot in her heart for ya, she got her own children's children to look after."

"Verna Bell, don't speak for me," Leola says. "I'm fine with Mary and her baby. Mary, you know that."

Verna Bell turns back to Mary. Persistent, she says, "Folks talk, Mary. You young and you strong. Lots of menfolk gon' have they eye on you. You can have your pick. Burt acted like he thought he was better'n the lot of 'em, but there's other good menfolk out here for you and that baby."

Mary pulls her gaze from little Houston's face and looks hard at her aunt.

When Verna Bell drops her eyes, Mary lets her own drift across the half-circle of women. "Ain't nobody 'round here worth half the salt Burt was," she says. She nuzzles her face against the baby's forehead.

"How about that John boy?" Hattie Mae says. "Now there's a man who's got his head fixed squarely on his shoulders."

"John Buckley?" Mary shrieks. "He old as dirt!"

The women laugh.

"Gal, he ain't that old," Verna Bell says, swatting at the air. "Humph. Not even forty yet. Plenty of women, young and old, carry on after him 'cause he got a good business head. Knows how to run a farm. Knows his place among white folks too."

Mary rolls her eyes. "Yeah, but it ain't his farm, it's the white man's farm, so what kind of power is that?"

"Power enough," Verna Bell says. "You got Burt's crazy talk all up in your head, and I understand it's gon' take some time to unravel all that. But this is the real world, gal. And you is somebody's mama now."

ON HER THIRD day after giving birth, Mary spends a few hours alone in her home. She is surprised at how at peace she feels being alone with the baby.

Delivering the baby had passed smoothly without complication or fanfare ("fair to middlin'" was Leola's assessment). One moment Mary's water was baptizing the threshold of her house; the next, she was in labor under the watch of Leola and the village midwife, and just two hours later, she was staring at the body of a ten-pound boy as the midwife held him over her.

Mary marvels at the persistence and innocence of new life.

"It's like it's two different worlds," she'd said later to Leola while staring into her son's face. "There's the world we know . . . and then there's the world this here child knows—safe and warm and full of milk. Which one more real?"

Leola had let out a sad, tired chuckle. "Oh, Mary, you and your questions! I dunno, child. I reckon they both is."

Away from the eyes of the other women—away from all their talk—Mary sits in her rocking chair for the first time and nurses Houston, feeling his deep tug on her nipple as he drains her of the milk that had been building up for this moment even when all she had wanted to do was die. As he suckles, Mary feels her nipple grow hot and then numb. She feels, also, an opening at the center of her. It is as deep and precise as a freshly dug grave, and it pulls on her too, trying to draw her into it, wanting to swallow her. But Mary is hungry now. For the first time in months, she feels ravenous. And you do not leave the table—or life—hungry. She yearns for turnip greens and corn-bread. She can see herself sopping the last corner of her bread in the greens' liquor. She wants field peas seasoned with ham hock, onion, and garlic sitting on top of a hill of buttered rice. She will pick every sliver of meat off her turkey neck bone. She will chew sautéed chicken gizzards forever. She will make gravy from flour and bacon drippings and pour it over every starchy thing. She will not waste away or crawl into the hole that wants to swallow her as much as her baby needs her.

Mary burrows her nose on the side of Houston's neck and inhales. She holds his new baby scent in her nostrils until she is forced to breathe again. She draws back and stares into his yellow-red face.

"We don't need nobody, do we?" she whispers, tracing his cheek with her finger. "Least, I don't need nobody."

The women had warned that she would grow lonely in the years to come. But Mary had loved and lost so much already that the threat of loneliness did not scare her. And because her body yearned for Burt's body only, she could imagine sleeping alone in its absence. She could imagine sleeping alone for the rest of her life.

But the baby.

Perhaps the ladies were right about Houston needing a father and about giving him a new life. He wouldn't even have to know about the past, they had said.

Mary marvels at how clear the baby's eyes are. She hopes his big bright eyes will never run across someone hanging from a tree. With the fervency of a fear that cuts even deeper, she moves her lips in silent prayer: *May you never find yourself hanging from a tree one day*. She pulls the baby tight against her, and he struggles, crying until she relaxes again.

We will have to leave Holmesville, Mary thinks. She can leave Holmesville now. No longer in a tug-of-war with Burt, no longer tied to the vision she had hoped to build with him here and had tested to see if he loved her enough to at least give it all he had, she is free to go.

CUTTING CORDS

FREEDOM IS DOLED OUT, or taken, in slices. We speak and write about it as though it is attainable as some whole and ever-lasting commodity. These days, to be child-free (as it had been for me) or marriage-free equals freedom. To be free of debt or the necessity of answering to a boss are others' ideas of freedom. For another, to flee America to a place where one's black body is not at risk of annihilation spells freedom.

But no one is fully free. What you believe you are fleeing pulls you back in some way, or you become reliant on it for your very livelihood. The one who sneers at motherhood ends up teaching as a profession, reliant upon the steady churning out of other people's children to sustain her career, or working in advertising that targets the purchasing power of families. The ex-patriot obsesses over what is going on in his birth country or finds himself entangled in tax issues his birth country won't let him easily absolve. The daring entrepreneur finds herself praying for investments from corporate backers and angel donors. And whites who believe they are free of the burden of being black or brown or that they are clean of racism carry, too, the ghosts of their ancestors. I have seen their ancestors flicker in their eyes.

What would Mary's life have been like if she had not married John Buckley? Marrying him and then leaving Mississippi offered one version of freedom—freedom from the scorn of being a single mother in those days and from the daily torture of tracing the steps she and Burt had walked together. That measure of freedom cost her something. All freedom costs something. All choices and perceived choices do.

MY MOTHER BELIEVED that by marrying my father she would gain the freedom to pursue her dreams. Since she was a young girl, her heart had been bent on traveling the world with her music. She wanted her guitar playing to anoint people, to save souls around the globe. That had been her prayer when she fasted and prayed in the attic at eleven.

"Lord, if you teach me how to play the guitar, I will use it to serve you," she prayed. When she came down from the attic, she told her parents, "I can play James's old guitar. I can play, Daddy!"

"Sure you can, baby," Papa Houston said.

"But I can. I really can. I prayed and fasted, and now I can play." The guitar was missing a string or two, but it had kept her connected to its owner and her favorite brother, James, who was serving in Vietnam.

When their daughter began to play her brother's instrument, her parents' mouths opened, and they were frozen. The sound coming from her fingers was beautiful and melodious—a miracle. The next day, Papa went down to the drugstore to put a new guitar on layaway for her, and over the next several years, he and Grandmama Avis did what they could to nurture their daughter's musical talent, which quickly included playing at the church.

They didn't know they were grooming her for an early marriage.

IT WAS 1970, the height of the Jesus movement, an evangelical Christian movement that took root in the West and spread across North America and beyond. It was a time of tent revivals and rented Hammond organs and souls being saved. My father, Donnell, was part of his family's traveling ministry, headquartered in his hometown of Beaumont, Texas, and free to roam under the guise of spreading the gospel. It was led by his eldest brother, a dynamic and charismatic man named Oscar Lane Jr. who could talk people into giving him whatever he wanted from them: instruments, the use of their talents and skills, money.

Mama didn't know that the country was in the midst of what would later be called a movement. She knew only that she loved the Book of Acts, loved reading about how the congregation was filled with the Holy Spirit on one accord, and she wanted to be likewise filled and anointed. She wanted her music to awaken souls in the congregation.

She and my father met in DeRidder during a revival taking place at St. Paul's Church down the street from our Elm Street house. As he beat the drums, Donnell eyed the slender girl with flawless, mud-brown skin, small eyes, and small white teeth. She was the most popular musician at the revival.

"A girl on the guitar?" people whispered.

She played her guitar as though she had been playing it forever, as though she were born playing it. After the service was over, Donnell cornered her.

What an ugly man, she thought when he first approached her. But his smile was handsome. He had big pearly teeth. And she liked the way he beat the drums. He told her his brother's band was going places. She had not been out of Louisiana but had always dreamed of seeing the world, particularly the three A's: Africa, Alaska, and Australia.

In between church services during the two-week revival, they stole moments to be together, telling each other their dreams. When it was time for my father's family to pack up and head to the next town or city, he asked her to marry him, and she, in the middle of her junior year of high school, said yes.

Several family members tried to talk some sense into her, but she did not listen. To her ears, their words of warning sounded like restriction.

Perhaps Grandma Mary was one of the elders who tried to dissuade her, but what, Pam must have thought, did she know? Besides, she had gotten pregnant with Houston before she and Burt were even married, and then he died, and she married a man she did not love. So what could she tell her about marriage and love and risk?

Grandmama Avis hurriedly transformed the plain den in her home into something beautiful, special, and memorable so that the wedding could take place there.

I can see them, Grandmama, Papa, and Grandma Mary, standing on the porch, their hearts swollen with fear, as my mother took off in caravans with strangers headed east first, they said, and then west. To freedom.

Today, I own the lace tablecloth—once white, now browned with age—that covered the buffet table at my parents' wedding ceremony. Grandmama's rush job in making the cloth is evident in the stitching that joins the wide swaths of lace and the cloth's solid center, but I doubt if Mama even noticed. She left the lace cloth behind after the wedding.

The summer after they married, my parents were participating in a revival in Portland when Mama discovered she was pregnant with me. But I was not destined to be born in the Pacific Northwest. Their stay in Portland was just three months before their next assignment in Camus, Washington, where, tired of Oscar Jr.'s controlling tactics, they quit the band and made their way back to Louisiana, passing through a hot, congested, and smoggy Los Angeles, where my mother gagged and wondered aloud, "Why would anyone want to live here?"

Little did she know that thirty years later, the daughter making her sick would make Los Angeles home. And while emission standards have decreased smog in LA, I still think of my mother when I am caught up in a web of traffic, especially one inching its way across the 110 Freeway where it runs through downtown Los Angeles. One day, I was behind a pickup truck that was carrying some kind of tar-making machine. The thick scent entered my nose and enveloped my esophagus, and I gagged. I pictured my mother's young, scrunched-up face.

My father would have liked nothing more, I imagine, than to stay in Los Angeles and try to make a go of it in Hollywood—doing whatever it took to garner fame: music, acting, comedy. He felt like a failure returning to my mother's hometown. Frustration, resentment, and unworthiness burned in his veins. Mama was eight months pregnant when he pounded his heavy fists into her back. She felt me shudder in her womb. A month later, I came out shaking. A nervous condition that would last.

She named me Cassandra Antoinette because she thought both names were French, and France was another place on her bucket list. She'd daydreamed of strolling in Paris, of easing freshly baked bread between her open lips.

Sixteen months after I was born, my sister was born. My father named her Lydia LaDena. Mama turned her head away when the midwife tried to hand Dena to her.

"Oh no, not another girl," she cried into her pillow. I consider her concern over having another girl in light of my fears of giving birth to a son. What was it, in those sixteen months of mothering me that made her dread the idea of another daughter? She was not a girl's girl; having grown up with brothers, girly things bored her, but perhaps her disdain was deeper than that. Perhaps she didn't want to be responsible for bringing another black girl child into this world where she would have to contend with not only an oppressive country but also, potentially, an oppressive mate. Or perhaps she didn't mean, "Oh no, not another girl." Perhaps she meant, "Oh no, not another baby."

I asked her once what she was thinking, how she was feeling, in those early years of conception and motherhood. I wanted to know if she had even wanted children, or if she'd wanted them later, after she was older and had realized some of her dreams.

"I won't be offended," I said. "I just want to know what was going through your mind. Where were you when you found out you were pregnant? How did you find out? What did you feel?"

She walked me through her actions but didn't open up the gates to her emotional world. I am the writer daughter, always brooding, always wanting more of what's under the surface, behind the first train of words, and this can be emotionally exhausting.

"I just remember missing that first period, and then missing it the second month and then, okay, by the third month I knew," she said. "I think I just called Mama. I didn't see a doctor. Didn't go to the doctor at all. I remember the sickness. I couldn't keep nothing down. I loved the flat we stayed in in Portland. Coming from DeRidder, from our old house and outhouse, that flat looked like a mansion. It had an inside bathroom with a clawfoot tub. During the pregnancy, your daddy was so abusive. I would soak in that water. Me and that tub became friends."

"How did you feel about everything, being pregnant and what was happening with your music?"

"I just remember feeling happy about the baby but hated that I wasn't home with Mama. Hated I had to tell her over the phone, but we weren't worried about what was next. No health insurance or nothing like that, but we didn't stress over it.

"When I got back to Louisiana, that's when I started seeing the midwife, Miss Shade. She did her own exams, and I had monthly visits with her. I remember her big old hands. She had some big old hands. My first pelvic exam was with her."

"So wonderful," I said, "that she was this black woman who owned her own business and helped birth so many of our relatives and friends."

"Yeah, she did. She opened up her own clinic. It was attached to her house. It was fifty dollars for me to have you, and seventy or seventy-five when Dena was born a year and a half later. Miss Shade was really nice, so friendly. She'd talk you through it. When I first went into labor, I was just a seventeen-year-old kid. I remember being in so much pain, so much pain. All of a sudden, I started saying, 'Lord, help me. Jesus, help me.' Miss Shade, she said, 'That's the one to call, baby,' and all of a sudden, the pain left, and I never had any more. All I felt was pressure; the Lord took that pain.

"You came into the world healthy, fine. Even your daddy was grinning and happy and crying. He was there when you and Dena both were born. Dena's umbilical cord was wrapped around her neck, but Miss Shade knew what to do, and she told him what to do. She told him to put his hands on my diaphragm area and push while she was pulling."

"Wow," I said, "I don't remember you ever telling me that part."

"No? I know your brain is always recording," she said. "I guess that's why I talk to you so much. I know you'll remember when the others won't. From a little kid, I could tell your little brain would be recording and taking in everything."

With this opening, I tried again to get at how she felt about becoming a mother so young and putting her own dreams on hold. She switched to third person, inserting distance.

"Moms, especially, always put their dreams later; that's what they do. Then a day passes, a year, years."

AFTER SHE LEFT my father, Mama moved into her old room and picked up her guitar again, pushing her nervousness into its strings. But in DeRidder, her music couldn't pay the bills. She landed her first job at Sears Roebuck taking catalog orders. While she was on shift one day, my father dropped by the house; he told Grandmama he wanted to spend some time with his daughters. She hesitated.

"Come on, Mother," he said. "I just want to take my girls out for a little shopping, buy them some ice cream." Instead, he drove us out of Louisiana, zipping past the Welcome to Texas sign, finally stopping at his mother's house in Beaumont.

"What I'm supposed to do with these girls, son?" his mother protested.

As his parents' middle child, my father had fought to prove himself. His siblings were becoming successful adults; he was the one everyone shook their heads at and asked, "What does Donnell have up his sleeve now?"

His mother was tall and had straight jet-black hair that swished against her lower back when she walked. In her presence, her sons and husband seemed to shrink.

My father stood looking helpless as his mother stared at him.

"It's Pam, Mother. She's trying to take my children and all my rights. If she calls, do me a favor and say you haven't seen me or these girls." His voice was squeaky and tight.

Dena and I huddled together behind him. We had not seen his mother often. She insisted we call her Grandmother, not Grandmama. Grandfather inched into the room; he had a permanent hump in his back. He smiled at us and patted the tops of our heads, keeping quiet as Grandmother instructed my father to stay someplace where he couldn't be found. While he didn't sleep in his parents' home, he was in and out while we were there. When he eventually called Mama, it was from a pay phone.

"Hello?" she answered. Her voice fell from the phone to the deserted street. "Hello? Donnell, is that you? Where are my children, Donnell? I've called the cops."

He didn't say anything, just pressed our mouths to the receiver.

"Mama! Mama!" we screamed, our cries joining hers.

Would we see her again? I wondered as my father hung up the receiver and pushed us back into the car.

Two weeks passed before his mother brought us back to DeRidder. She dropped us off at a supermarket and called our mother to pick us up. She had plaited our hair and reminded us to keep our backs straight when we stood or walked.

Our father returned to DeRidder, begging and crying and explaining to us that he'd been so scared of losing us, that he loved us.

"Don't say you love me, Donnell, 'cause you don't," Mama said. "If we do get back together, don't let me hear you say that word again because you don't know what it means." She went back to him, and they tried to start over in a little yellow-framed white house on Branch Street.

On warm days, they stayed inside their bedroom where the box fan was the only sound coming through the closed door. Outside, Dena played hide-and-seek with children in the neighborhood as I gathered rocks that looked like caramels and buried them in the backyard.

My father wanted to go back to Beaumont, but Mama told him she wasn't leaving DeRidder again, that she wouldn't get in a car with him behind the wheel. A month later, after a loud argument, she left him again. She stuffed our few clothes and toys into trash bags and slung them into the backseat of the blue Buick she had borrowed from Papa Houston.

On one of her trips to the car, my father locked Dena and me inside the house with him and one of his friends. The tall,

146

menacing man stood over us with a long, leather belt. Trudging up the hill leading back to the house, Mama heard our hollering. She tried to get in through the front door, but it was locked. She ran to one of the side windows and succeeded in opening it and sticking her head in before my father rushed over and let the window slide down.

She barely escaped what looked to me like a guillotine.

Through the window, I saw the pain on her twenty-three-year-old face and the silver that had started multiplying in her hair during her seven-year hell with my father.

Outside, fighting off Mama's attempts to grab us, my father and his friend carried Dena and me to a car. Somehow, Mama got Dena. But his friend snatched open the door and threw me onto the back seat just as my father started the ignition. Mama was hanging onto the door of the car when he pressed the accelerator hard and zoomed off. Through the back window, I saw her body rolling on the ground, dangerously close to the mouth of a deep, concrete-filled ditch.

She lived, as I discovered several hours later. My father had decided he didn't want me after all. He dropped me off on Elm Street and left. He threw a party that night in the Branch Street house. He got drunk and carried on about how thrilled he was that we were gone. He danced long and hard with a woman who later stabbed him with an ice pick. He survived that and more, though. He was destined, he said, to make the big time, to be somebody.

Even when he was free of us, however, he didn't rush off to Hollywood.

Late one night, he pried open a window at our house and climbed in. A heavy scent of liquor invaded Mama's bedroom.

"You think you can leave me and take my kids?" He stumbled toward Mama, who had jumped up from her bed.

"Donnell, what're you doing in here?"

"You think you're something, PamaJean, don't you? Got that sorry ass job. You think you're something now, but you ain't nothing."

"You the one who ain't nothing, Donnell," Mama yelled back. "Coming in here like this."

Papa Houston appeared, holding his rusted shotgun in his thick hands. "You better leave, boy, before I have to use this," he said.

Mama alerted our elementary school's principal that my father might do something crazy, and he promised to keep an eye on us.

Calling her by her maiden name, the principal, Mr. Blunt, a dark-skinned black man whose perfect small afro glistened every day, told her, "Your girls are safe here, Miss Buckley."

Papa and Grandmama's house was only a short walk away, but my first-grade teacher, Mrs. Meadows, drove Dena and me home every day after school.

Once, during lunch, my father strode into the cafeteria, wearing a black cowboy hat and cowboy boots. The girls at my table giggled.

"Oh my God, he looks like a movie star," one squealed.

Frightened of him and what he might do, I was confused because as the girls nudged each other and pointed, I felt pride. Popular. Tightening my shoulders to keep from shaking, I barely moved my lips in a whisper: "That's my daddy."

The girls' eyes widened and sparkled. "Your daddy?"

My father came over to my table and sat down.

"There's my girl," he said, but then turned away from the fear in my eyes. He joked with the other kids, making faces as he pretended to eat their food.

Mr. Blunt ran into the cafeteria. "Sir, you're not supposed to be here."

"I just wanted to see my girls," my father told the principal, flashing him a wide grin. "Is there any harm in that?"

"Sir, you need to leave."

He left the school, and after that, he left DeRidder. We rarely saw him. He called one Christmas with promises.

"Babies, your daddy's got a truckload of toys for y'all. It'll only take me an hour to get from Beaumont to DeRidder. You know how fast your daddy drives." He laughed and laughed.

Every time we heard an engine, Dena and I ran to the living room and pressed our faces against the screen door. When darkness fell and the streetlight popped on, he still had not come. We cried ourselves to sleep.

As we came of age, despite how much we believed we were going in the other direction, we are our mother's daughters. We were both in and out of relationships, searching for sweetness and forever. At least Mama, the youngest child and only daughter, was the apple of her father's eye. She left home early but left a home base filled with love. She could hold each of her relationships with men up against the scale of how her father treated her: with love and adoration and respect. My sister and I did not have that. And since Papa Houston belonged squarely to Mama, Burt Bridges became the father figure of my imagination. The one I deserved. He did not willingly leave me.

They took him.

THE DASH TO Mama's gospel music and travel dreams was devastating. Still, no matter what she endured over the years, she always eventually found her way back to her guitar. She played after her marriage ended and between babies and broken romances and long work hours. She played at home and in churches. She was playing from our living room on the evening of my first kiss.

My first boyfriend, DosReis, and I were standing outside under the acorn tree. It covered us like a waterfall as we tiptoed over acorns, looking into and away from each other's eyes, knowing what was next. At sixteen, my lips were still virgin lips.

They had not yet pressed against those of a boy. My tongue had not yet moved over to make room for another's tongue; it had not rolled over and under that moist muscle, trading saliva and breath.

He leaned in and pressed his purple-brown lips to mine—full and pink with a cherry gloss. I was surprised by how easily he entered my mouth, how readily it spread. And I tasted the sweet soil of him—of man. We were all lips and tongues and saliva and heartbeats while the sound from Mama's amplified electric strings floated from the living room, filtered through the screen door, and spilled onto the yard. The leaves shivered. We held on, and we dreamed of forever.

"IN A FEW WEEKS, we'll be doing what it took to get your mom's belly big," DosReis whispered to me as we sat on the porch one night.

"No, we will not" is what I should have said; instead, I lifted my face to his. I watched his perfect white teeth strain against his skin as he grinned. I was in love with his dimples, the dip in his chin, and his small and sparkling eyes.

"What do you mean?" I asked, feigning innocence, with just a smudge of sensuousness and softening my eyes like I imagined the heroines doing in Mama's romance novels.

DosReis's prophecy came to pass our senior year of high school. After junior prom, we had sex for the first time but used a condom. Overcome with guilt and pain, I crawled into a fetal position under the hotel's sink and cried as I rested my thin, curled limbs against the sink's cold, hollow pipes. DosReis stood just outside the bathroom, frozen with confusion, I'm sure, but the sight of him standing there, frigid with fear or uncertainty or whatever it was, made me cry harder. The pipes were hard and unyielding. Judging.

"Look at you," they said. "You've given yourself to this boy, and he doesn't even know how to fill you back up." With what? I had no idea. But touch, whispered reassurances, tears of his own—anything would have been better than the dark and distant outline he made at the door's threshold.

Over the next year, our sex got better. I even began to enjoy it, and we fooled around with condoms and without.

When I missed my period, I kept all my hysteria between DosReis and me. Marie's words rang in my ears, except I imagined her replacing the pronoun: "Haven't you ever heard of the word *condom*? How could you get pregnant at the same time as your own mother?"

I was stupid, I kept scolding myself, to have felt so confident in DosReis's promises to pull out. I had dreams, and he had dreams. We were going to college. We were going to be professionals.

If I had the baby, there would be three generations of mamas in our house. Grandmama had raised her clan of eight long ago, but there she was in old age dealing with her grandchildren and witnessing her daughter being burdened by her choices, and marked by frowns, stretched skin, and her brothers' scorn.

"Fornication is a sin," Uncle Junior, leader of our new family church, Faith Mission, would say during service.

Mama, after playing her guitar during the praise segment, would be sitting right on the front row of the congregation, her belly swollen, and her head downturned. She didn't say anything to Uncle Junior, but later at home, she would complain to Grandmama about other folks in town who were whispering behind her back.

"I haven't been with many men," she would say. "Seems like every few years that I am with somebody, I wind up pregnant. People don't care about you fornicating unless a baby comes out of it."

Grandmama was her best and most loyal friend. She would

rub her daughter's hair or hold her hand; her support was silent and strong. As the tears fell, Grandmama listened.

"Seems like what they're really saying is that sex outside of marriage isn't a sin until a baby is coming," I overheard my mother saying one day. "Long as there's no child, long as there's no evidence."

I did not want to be the recipient of the town's scorn.

I had the abortion on a bright and cool Saturday in October of 1988. The annual Beauregard Parish fair was in town, and DosReis and I told our parents that we were going to the fair. He borrowed his stepfather's navy-blue Lincoln ("the hearse," we called it), but instead of driving up town, we cobbled our after-school job money together and drove across the Louisiana state line and into Beaumont, where my father lived.

DosReis parked the Lincoln at the She Clinic, and we went in. A thin white woman in the waiting room leaned in close to me. She fixed her jumpy bright brown eyes onto mine for a few seconds.

"Don't worry," she said, grinning. "It doesn't hurt a bit. This is my fifth one."

I didn't care about the pain. My brain and body were numb with determination.

The mask of gas the doctor gave me filled me with hollows of laughter. I laughed and laughed and laughed. My bellows rang through the halls, creeping up DosReis's spine. There were pricks along my own spine; deep tickles circled in my throat and settled in my belly. If there were a reactionary cringing in my uterus, if life tried to hang on to life, I do not recall; I was disconnected from it. I had programmed my brain for this mission.

I had made a mistake; *we* had made a mistake, I told myself. And we just had to fix it. And I had to fix it without anyone besides the two of us knowing. I would proudly wear my badge of freedom from motherhood. I would not have children. I could not have children. I would not bear the burden of my foremothers. I could not bear the burden of my foremothers. Their lives had been heavy, stunted, repetitive.

At seventeen, I believed I was destined to be different—destined for freedom.

"You are my rock, Sand," Mama often said to me, and I cannot count how many women have said this to me, or something along its lines, over the years.

You are my rock.

But I was not and am not a rock. I am, in name and reality, Sand: a crumbly and unstable thing.

In my mother's hospital room, I held my youngest little brother Dane and swayed like a softly pushed swing.

"He's not ugly at all," I said after some time. While I regarded his father with disdain, I was surprised at the immediate love I felt for my baby brother. His father had promised to marry Mama, had bought her an engagement ring, and then abandoned her when she told him she was pregnant.

"I'll put you and the kids up in a house, but I'm not marrying you," he said.

I hated his voice—how thick and slurring and arrogant it was.

"You had babies for those other niggas; you can have mine."

"I refuse to be one of your kept women," Mama told him.

After she and the baby came home, she kept herself sequestered in her room, the same room she had slept in as a girl; it was the space we gathered in with her for intimate moments around a TV show or talk and felt barred from at other times when she was in the height of anger or lows of depression.

By trying so hard not to be like my mother, had I altered my true nature?

Was she wrong for wanting love and marriage? Was I?

WHEN I VISIT my mother as an adult, I inevitably find myself in her music room, where multiple guitars rest in stands in the middle of the small space. I pick one up and place it across my lap. It hurts to feel the weight of it under my breast now that my mother's chest will never be the same. Her life is light-years away from the one she had as a teenager, marrying and leaving home. In Florida, she remarried, giving love a chance yet again after so many broken romances; she bought her first home, where she is surrounded by more than an acre of land. For a time, she enjoyed playing her guitar for audiences again at the House of Blues at Disney World while she was part of a gospel band. But her body, in so many ways, gave out on her just as she was finding her stride again. She had double bypass heart surgery some years ago. The surgeon had to break open her sternum, and her chest still echoes with pain. I can recall her cradling her instrument at her breasts as much as I can seeing them plump up with milk for a baby sibling. After she weaned each baby, I watched her breasts revert to their natural state— small and perky—ready again to sit above one of her guitars.

My fingers fumble over strings that might as well be her fingers, her cells. I am awkward here. This is not my instrument, and yet as her firstborn, I cannot help but wonder how often my suckling baby self kept her from it. I feel responsible. How awkward I must have felt, moist and squirmy, in place of the hard smooth back of her guitar. How did her arms look holding me instead of the left one stretched out to clasp her guitar's neck and the right one crooked over its arched body, snug and sure?

TO CARRY LIFE AND DEATH

I LIKE TO get up before dawn when the morning is blacker than midnight. When the air is still but not silent. When the birds are so loud, you'd swear I was in the woods instead of this uber-urban South Los Angeles neighborhood, where, in about an hour or so after my rising, the main thoroughfare bustles with traffic and the inevitable siren. A parade of old storefronts—liquor marts, barber and beauty shops, a shoe shop, a teeny church, a fish market—stand at attention along stained sidewalks, mirroring the scene of a thousand streets in so-called hoods across the United States.

Here, though, the scenery changes in a few short minutes as you swoop up onto the hill where the buildings loom larger and where, just beyond their shoulders, the houses are large and lush, too, in an area that is nicknamed the "Black Beverly Hills." Down here in the flats, aging men hurry to the liquor stores and linger around their doors. A homeless man in a wheelchair is tucked into his usual spot outside a vacant building.

My street is located just around the corner from all that. It is a street lined with stucco bungalows, some of which have been remodeled and freshly painted, while others bear the hues and textures of a bygone trend. Inside the fading salmon hue of one such bungalow, while Marcus slept, I would close myself off in the little room that I claimed as my writing room. I would go in before having to get ready to head out to a nearby high school to teach composition, literature, and journalism. This room was my cocoon. Amber incense burned, string lights draped my bookcase, and my space heater hummed. My body electric and aware, I would aim my senses and imagination to hear the pulse of my past, my ancestors, my baby.

In my fourth month, after raking through a dozen options, Marcus and I chose a name for our baby.

Carmen.

"I've always loved the name Carmen," I told him.

"Me too," he said. "There's something so sweet about it. And all the important women in my life have names that start with C."

I rattled off the part of his history I knew out loud: Creola, his centenarian great-grandmother; Cosette, his beloved late grandmother; Charmaine, his mother; Carol, the name of his ex-wife before she changed it to Alchemy; and me, Cassandra.

Carmen.

"It's so rich and smooth sounding in the mouth. Carmen. Carrr-mennnn." I said it over and over again.

"Okay, Carmen it is then," Marcus said. "Now we just need to come up with her middle name."

My excitement over the baby was overshadowed by illnesses. As each week passed, heartburn pain and PUPPP rashes intensified. Marcus tried to ease my discomfort with creams from the drugstore and homemade remedies he found on the internet. Nothing helped. (I take that back. Snapping at him when he asked me if I was feeling better—that did help a little.)

The only deep cravings I had were for salad (vinegary, crunchy, and topped with green olives), Krispy Kreme doughnuts (Marcus had to make a 2 a.m. run to the one in the Crenshaw District once), and fresh figs. I would comb the produce sections in search of figs that looked dark enough to hold at least a measure of the sugar the figs of my childhood held.

Then, figs were free. On Elm Street, our fig trees were my covering—thick, wide-palmed leaves provided shade for me while I stretched out on a quilt, while I read, and animated the clouds.

The fig—with its strange, plump body, with its complicated texture—is everything to me: love, scripture, discovery, sensuality. And my body craved figs constantly. I wished I could walk out the back door, take a few steps to Grandmama's grove of fig trees, and pick to my heart's—and stomach's—content.

I WORRIED ABOUT carrying something that was alive and delivering it not alive. Perhaps it was leftover trauma from the abortion, perhaps leftover trauma from Grandma Mary and who knows what other ancestors, but the fear of carrying dead things and not knowing it has, I believe, been with me ever since I was a girl and heard the story of how Grandmama Avis's first baby was stillborn.

This is how I imagined it:

Avis pushed her first baby's body out into the world and knew right away that she had given birth to a dead thing.

The midwife looked up at Avis with tired and sorrowful eyes. Avis felt a vast ache in her womb.

"Let me hold him," she pleaded with the midwife. She wanted to smell his hair, his skin—that new baby smell. As the midwife washed him up a little, fear tore at the emptiness that had spread inside Avis, stabbing it like a sharp knife. Would he smell like death? Would she be able to scrub that stench from her nostrils, or would it follow her the rest of her life?

When she held him, he smelled like nothing—or else she held her breath for the length of time he was in her arms. She held him tight, cupped to her neck, but he was like a doll baby in her arms, slight and lifeless. It struck her that this is what she knew about having her own baby: nine months of waiting and then bereft still for all the moments she had dreamed about: the scent of his hair, the life in his eyes, and the feel of his heartbeat outside her own body.

She had eight children after that. With each one, she waited for death to beat her over the head again. When it failed, she would sink her nose into each baby's fuzzy head. There were years when she didn't know how their growing family was going to make it, but she was grateful her children were alive, that they were all alive together.

SALT CRAVING

IN ONE OF my earliest memories, I am five years old and standing on the inside of an opaque, mustard-colored curtain. The curtain, designed for living rooms, hangs from my bedroom window. The underside of the cloth is coated, resembling the meat of a coconut. I hide my body from my family but not from the world outside my window. Can they see me? It is late evening. A violet haze lingers a few frozen moments before darkness falls completely. That is where I am caught.

With my skirt pulled down to my ankles, I press myself against a feather-stuffed pillow and mentally block out the ruckus in the front part of the house: Mama screaming. My sister crying. My father slamming the front door.

I shudder, collapsing against the pillow.

EACH ORGASM IS likened to a little death, I learned many years later after I understood what my body was giving me: an avenue to escape, an avalanche of pleasure that, in those few seconds, could numb my fears and fill in the gaps of my longing for security, love, and peace. When I was five, my mother was only twenty-two. She had not yet experienced an orgasm. My father's approach to sex was selfish and abrasive. I cannot recall witnessing a single moment of intimacy between them. They had no idea how critical such a display of affection was to their children's development.

BEFORE I STARTED kindergarten, before I learned to spell my name correctly, my father taught me how to draw. He started me off tracing comic-strip characters until I could create, free-hand, Snoopy's nose just so. It wasn't fun; it was meticulous: Draw a line. Erase it. Start over. My neck and fingers would ache. Afraid to complain, I began to savor the softness of my father's breath behind my ear and the warmth of his large fingers closing over my tiny ones.

After Mama left him, I was often afflicted with constipation, nausea, and dizziness. I let empty spaces embrace me. Mama would find me tucked away in some corner, playing alone or staring into what to her was emptiness. One afternoon, she found me, small and unconscious and nude, in the blue-gray light of the bathroom, flat on my back in the tub.

"Lord, my child," she yelled.

Grandmama came running, wrapped me in one of the tattered bath towels, and anointed me with blessed virgin olive oil, the smell of which turned my stomach upside down. She prayed over my limp body and then got me to stand and raise my arms to the rain-stained ceiling, thanking God for his mercy.

"We couldn't get you to eat anything but greens," Mama told me years later.

The greens, I can taste now. I taste them the way Grandmama used to cook them before Papa's diabetes and her high blood pressure set in. They would be full of salt and pepper, the flavor of salted pork embedded in their wilted green-black leaves. Turnips were my favorite greens; they absorb salt more fully.

Mama got used to finding me in the tub, and if no greens had been cooked, she would ask Grandmama to put on a pot so that I could get something in my stomach.

"That girl had one of her heat spells again," she'd announce and pull me up.

She didn't take me to a doctor until boils rose on the back of my neck, filled with pus and blood. She and Grandmama prayed over me first and wondered if the abscesses had anything to do with the matches Grandmama had caught me eating a few weeks before. As if they were candy, I had sucked the red heads of the matches until the grains melted into my tongue.

When Grandmama saw me, I had eaten dozens of the little heads and placed the pale, wooden sticks back into the fat box that sat on top of the den's heater. I don't know what made me put the first match tip into my mouth, whether I had sensed the salty taste would be there. The acrid, chemical taste of the matches was unpleasant and irritating but a sacrifice I was willing to pay for the salt.

Every now and then, I crave the taste of matches. The saltiness, the pungency, the smell of sulfur hangs between the roof of my mouth and nasal cavity even now. The inbred desire for salt never left me. Give me salt and heat, and I am sustained. I was drawn to the matches and to the fire leaping behind the bricks in our heaters. These were not pyromaniacal desires; I wanted only to draw them both into my body—the salt and the heat—to warm me, to keep me alive.

I've heard of people who are love starved becoming addicted to sugar. I was separated from my father, whose love I didn't feel even when we were with him. But my need for salt may have been a crying out for him as he was in all his spiciness and abrasiveness.

WHEN WE REACHED our teens, Dena and I begged Mama to let us go to Texas. We wanted to know who our father was behind the monster of our early childhood memories, beyond the lies and neglect. How did he live his daily life? Over the years, Mama had fed us the harsher stories of him; still, he was a part of us and we of him. Surely there was something good that linked us?

"Go ahead," she said, struggling to hide her fear and feelings of betrayal. "Go on and let that man fill you with his fantasies and lies."

Through older eyes, I realized Beaumont is not the big city he promised he'd wind up in. It's the medium-sized town in which he grew up with a houseful of siblings and responsibilities.

My father and his second wife had a son who was eight years my junior—my brother, a stranger. The three of them lived in a brick house on a street called Sunnydale. As Dena and I crossed the threshold, my father turned with a grin to see our eyes widen. Their place was decorated with plush carpet, animal-print throws, and brass statues. I was impressed, but hoped instead that my face revealed the disgust I felt that he was living this lavishly when we'd been living all those years in my grandparents' decaying house.

He had told Mama one day as they were screaming at each other through the phone, "PamaJean, those girls ain't gonna get one copper cent from me."

He'd kept that promise.

In the garage of his home were electronics and appliances of all kinds, things he said he repaired and sold for a living. Mama figured it was some sort of cover-up for one of his latest scams. It was true, at least, that he had been in and out of jail for some illegal attempt or another to strike it rich.

Pointing to a white pickup truck with Don's TV Repair and Sales painted on the side, he bragged, "Babies, at least your daddy don't work for the man."

During a gathering of extended family—a few of his siblings and their kids—he showed us a videotape of himself on stage at a talent show trying to crack up the audience with a stand-up act chock-full of clichés. Guffawing at his own jokes, he seemed oblivious to the quiet in the auditorium, even to the embarrassment on the faces in his living room.

I told him I was preparing to go to college, that I was going to write for newspapers, and one day write books.

"Ha! Ain't that something." His wide mouth opened even wider in a loud laugh. He boasted to the rest of the family that I had taken after him. He rushed from the room, coming back with shoeboxes of scripts he said he had written.

He said one was soon to be turned into a movie. The glitter in his eyes led me to think he believed it.

"I'm gonna make it, girls. Your daddy's gonna make it."

We didn't look at his face. We looked at each other, our eyes passing a silent, "Yeah, right."

A few seconds later, I caught a glimpse of the scribbled-on scraps of paper shaking in his hand, and for the first time, I pictured him as a young man filled with hope for a better life, a life filled with prosperity and excitement and relevance. For the first time, I saw him as vulnerable.

My insides trembled with him.

THERE IS A tremor at the center of me that has never fully erupted, only threatens to erupt. I feel it most when I am angry or nervous; for example, when I have to speak or read publicly. It starts in my stomach, radiates to the tips of my fingers, and shivers down to my knees.

Once, I was reading an essay in front of an audience at the Tennessee Williams Festival in New Orleans. My mother was visiting me that weekend. She sat in the front row. I had made the mistake of wearing a dress.

"Your voice was strong," Mama said later, "but when I looked down and saw the hem of your skirt shaking, I thought, 'My poor baby!'"

I hope one day to not be so shaky, so overrun by emotions

that my body threatens to crumble, but I do not know how to heal the injuries that originate in the womb: wounds of slavery, lynching, and domestic violence.

I AM LEARNING that no matter how much you want to divorce yourself from your past—or from one of your parents—both are intrinsically part and parcel of you for the rest of your life. My father's ways colored my sister's ways and mine long after Mama left him and reentered the home and culture of her youth.

On my mother's side, we were a black and sanctified people who believed in hard work and God. While secular music was forbidden in our home, its beats surrounded Dena and me every time we stepped outside our house, and those beats felt as though they had always been a part of my blood and marrow.

Our school bus driver, Mr. St. Romaine, blasted R&B over the speakers on the way to and from school. He raised the volume to drown out the students' noise. His music eased his scowl. I got lost in the lyrics and rhythm of the Isley Brothers' "Insatiable Woman." I didn't exactly know what the song meant, but my body responded to its suggestiveness.

We were late bloomers, Dena and I. We were well into our teens before any sign of womanhood began to peek through our stick bodies and before what the world would deem as desirable began to flower.

In the afternoons, we would sneak on MTV and VH1 whenever we could, watching Janet Jackson move her hips and flip her hair over her eyes. On Saturdays, Mama would drop us off at the washateria before she drove off toward more errands or to return home to rest. There was a jukebox inside the laundry mat, and we relished opportunities to listen to the latest R&B and pop hits on blast. We especially loved Klymaxx's "Meeting in the Ladies Room" and all of Jody Watley's hits. Dena swore she was Jody Watley. She teased and sprayed her hair, donned enormous hoop earrings, and (when liberated from our family's watchful eyes) painted her lips red.

When Salt-N-Pepa's "Push It" came on, we lost it. After a few Saturdays of getting our routine down, we ran outside to the concrete walkway in front of the washateria one day, dancing away all semblance of shyness. We bent our knees and gyrated our hips. Left, right. Right, left.

Mama would have fainted. Then promptly risen and whipped our behinds.

We had never seen our mother dance, nor our grandparents, although Grandmama was prone to a sudden foot shout now and then to a gospel song at church, on the record player, or one locked in her head.

To what were Dena and I grinding? Why did our bodies yearn to move despite what we had been taught? How had our pelvises known how to move?

We are our father's daughters.

As we blossomed into teenagers, Mama tried to prepare us for impending romantic heartache. Her prophecies were as doomful as the ones Uncle Junior handed down in church about the end times.

"Men will use you up and throw you away," she would say.

We had seen her attempt to date since leaving our father in the late seventies; we had seen her left high and dry and pregnant when those men threw her away. To make matters worse, she said, black men always want white women or the next best thing: a combination of big breasts, long flowing hair, and light skin. The lighter the better.

I had none of that.

My skin was the color of maple syrup, my breasts shaped like small cones, and my hair coarse and slow to grow.

Still, when I got ready for love, I was determined to prove

Mama wrong. There are great black men out there, I thought, and I would find my black knight. I would not be like her, choosing the wrong man over and over. I had to believe I was as worthy, as sexy, and as beautiful as the women I looked nothing like. And I had to believe there were men who would appreciate me the way I was. More than that, I had to believe that there was one who would make me, as the group Midnight Star sang, the object of desire.

I LOVE MEN, but I had seen my mother and other women broken too many times by the men they loved. But while a part of me fought against those narratives and held out hope and belief that true love and true fidelity between a black man and a black woman were possible—yes, like in Mama's romance novels but with our own twist—I still had something to prove. I wanted to demolish every single lie that black men had ever told themselves about me, about black women; I wanted to get inside that lie, to the belly of it, which means I have had to get inside the man, inside his head and heart and trust because the surefire, most effective way to uproot what has had time to nest is to dig down to the beginning of the network of roots. I wanted to get into the center of the lies and plant dynamite and then crawl back out to safety and watch the devastating lies explode and burn and turn to ash. The lies I want to destroy are that we, black women, are strong enough to withstand their bullshit and weak enough to take them back; that we are too much while simultaneously not enough; that we are backward and gullible, stubborn and difficult; and that we will always be there no matter what, even if they leave.

I've wanted loyalty, but what is loyalty to me? I am willing to love black men as hard as they love me, for as long or as short as that fuse burns; when it goes out, I have no clue how to light it back.

WITH WIDE SWATHS of years existing between the moments my father and I communicate, I have been, mostly, able to forget about him, to forget I have a father, and perhaps this ability to shut off a valve in my heart colors my relationships with men. And yet when out of the blue my father does reappear in my life—through a letter or Facebook message—I find it hard to breathe. The closed-off valve in my heart pumps again, waiting for him to redeem himself, to declare his undying love, to say, "I'm sorry."

That has never happened, and I am left with the task of closing the valve back up again and packing it with ice. Yet as I carried my child, his grandchild, in my body, I realized I no longer hated my father. Trying to protect my child from ancestral trauma outside of my control might have been an impossible feat, but what I could control, I believed, was the effect of my father's baggage on my parenting.

I searched for the few photos I have of my father and studied them, studied his young face. All of the images are from the early seventies. In one, he is sitting in a gold jacquard-print armchair. He has on a black, nylon, collared shirt with small white buttons; gray slacks; sheer black socks; and a shiny silver watch with a gold-trimmed face. He has placed the fingers of his left hand on his chin for a kind of contemplative pose. His smile is slight, seeking confidence—glamour even. His short fro is immaculate. His appearance stands out against the stark and sparse background: bare walls, cheap brown carpet, and a large whirring box fan. How hot was it that day, and where was my father going or coming from?

In this photo, he is a new father. I am one year old, and my sister Dena is on the way.

As I stare at the image, it strikes me that I've never seen a photograph of my father as a child—vulnerable, hopeful—and that missing image feels vital. Did someone crush his spirit, and if so, at what point? Was it someone he knew and trusted? How did his country put its knee on his black neck and at what point? When he was a teen or younger?

Surely, he was not always a perpetually tormented soul who wreaks havoc on other souls.

When I first moved to Los Angeles, he got my mailing address from Dena and sent me a large brown envelope filled with homemade greeting cards he had drawn and written something he called poetry on. He was in jail.

"Your daddy loves you," he wrote.

I wondered, Who is the me that he loves? Suddenly, my sense of self was swallowed. Perhaps he knew me in a way that I did not know myself. Perhaps there was some part of me out there being loved by him and the me I knew was completely detached from her. His poetry was candy-cane sweet—the purple-and-yellow candy canes that I once gorged on so much as a kid that the very sight of them today makes my stomach queasy.

I wrote him back, telling him how the pain of his absence had stifled me for years. I told him about my choice not to become a mother.

In his response letter, he laughed at me. He ignored the pain I revealed and laughed. At least, his words, haughty and confident, felt like laughter.

"You will have children," he wrote. "You will have many children, my daughter."

I read the lines again and again. Shaken. Furious. Unsure.

ON OUR WAY to Houston once, a man I was dating suggested we stop in Beaumont to see my father. John was from Houston and was taking me to meet his family. He was of the belief that families should be reconciled. He wanted to do the honorable thing and meet my father.

"Maybe he's changed," he said, full of empathy for my father: another man.

"Yeah, right," I said. "I doubt it."

I was twenty-four, carving out a life for myself, and a part of me wanted my father to see what he had missed in not raising me, not caring. I had graduated from high school and college without him, and I was working my first full-time job as a newspaper reporter. My boyfriend was a pleasant young man who was climbing the corporate ladder. I wanted my father to see all of this and be proud—and ashamed.

But I watched him look at me and see only himself. He brought out shoeboxes of poems and stories and jokes he had written.

"I've been writing for years," he said after I told him that I worked as a journalist. "I could give you a run for your money."

I never got around to telling him about my larger dreams. He provided no space.

"Maybe you could take some of my stories back with you, show some of your people," he said. "Baby, your daddy gon' be famous."

"I'm so sorry, babe," my boyfriend said when we were back in the car. "It was a mistake to come here." His big hands were warm on my face. He kissed my tears and I laughed.

"I told you," I said. "You wanted me to come here. Put the past in the past, right?"

"I'm so sorry," he repeated.

And I was sorry, too, in that moment, as well as a year or so later when I broke John's heart. His soft words turned to stones that he threw.

"My mama warned me about girls like you. Girls with no daddies," he spat at me when I told him I was in love with someone else, an older man. Ric.

What is loyalty to me? I have never seen it up close. I hold out hope that Mary and Burt were the epitome of loyalty and love and that all we as a family needed was to be witnesses of that love.

Perhaps my obsession with Burt Bridges really is just a search for a father.

I want a father who is good and great and alive.

I want a love that is good and great and alive.

MARY AND BURT, 1904

IN ALL HER days of knowing him, Mary realizes, Burt was never satisfied.

"Look around," she recalls him telling her once when they were sitting on the step of the uneven porch to their misshapen square of a house. "This here a shack we livin' in, Mary,"

Mary was offended. "Yeah, but it's ours," she said.

"All the colored folks we know living in shacks, some of the white ones, too, but not all of 'em."

"It might be a shack," Mary said, "but I make it home, Burt." She was thinking of the woods that backed up the house, a forest of green that she could not, back then, ever imagine leaving. She grew up learning those woods, their scents and sounds, and the way they captured and held the waxing and waning light of the sun and moon.

She looked at Burt. "You know how to make ugly pretty too," she said. She pointed with her eyes to the flower beds he had planted for her, to her rose bushes, to the grass with its glowing yellow inside blades of green. She looked over at the strawberries running along the partial fence, the vines of jasmine and honeysuckle winding around the posts just above the berries. "But pretty is in the eye of the beholder, I reckon," she said to Burt, trying not to sound petulant but failing.

He shrugged as his eyes flittered over the plants and their fruit; his mind was far away.

Mary called him back to her with a tease. "Hey man, do you think I'm pretty? Or am I just a pile of rags to you too?"

She had intended it to come off flirty and flip, but Burt saw the shadows in her eyes, the uncertainty, the real question squirming beneath the playfully confrontational one. He ran his eyes over her face: her wide, wary eyes; high cheekbones; and broad, softly squared jaw. Her face was smooth and dark, like the polish he used to shine his best shoes, like the color of roasted coffee beans—where brown meets black, a magical shade. Her nose was strong at the bridge before flowing into nostrils that curved out like her hips, soft and firm. Her hair was plaited back into cornrows, leaving her high forehead as open as the sky. He followed her hairline down to her ears, perfectly shaped lobes exposed by her cornrows. His eyes fell to her long neck and down to her breasts, her waist and hips, her shapely calves.

Mary shifted her body under his gaze. "Well, what's your final appraisal, sir?"

Burt grinned with lopsided lips. "You know what my ma used to always tell us?"

"What's that?"

"She used to say"—he looked into Mary's eyes—"she used to say God don't like ugly, and he don't care too much about pretty either."

They laughed together.

"You know you a mighty fine woman to me."

"Why thank ya, kind sir. I may be a little rough around the edges, 'cause I know how to do hard work, but I care about pretty. I take this life and this face and this body—what's been given me—and I try to make it as pretty as I can. I don't ask nobody for nothing. Your problem is you want too much, Burt, and that want can get you into a heap o' trouble."

Burt had grabbed his head with both hands and rocked his

upper body back and forth as he groaned. "Oh, Mary, Mary. You sound just like my pa. Accept, accept, accept. What if all this is a test, Mary? You black folks always talking 'bout what God wants for us, but what if He is testing us? What if God is thinking who gon' be down for the fight, and who gonna lay down and take what they been given?"

Mary sighed, rolling her eyes at this argument she'd heard over and again. "Burt, ain't nobody layin' down nothing. We just ain't all as high-minded as you."

Old Sarge bounded from around the back of the house and sauntered up to Burt, laying his big floppy head over his owner's feet.

"See there?" Mary said. "Even Old Sarge is telling you to stay put. Hold your horses, man."

Burt bent over to ruffle the dog's head. "You think that's what he saying, huh woman? Naw. I think what he thinking is, "Massah, massah, don't leave me. Take me with you and leave this hardheaded woman behind."

Mary jumped up from the step and flung herself onto Burt's lap. "Massah, massah," she said, echoing the singsong of Burt's voice. "Please don't leave me behind. Take me with you. Whatever you do, I do. Where ever you go, I go."

Burt leaned his head back and squinted his eyes as he took in hers, alight now with pure mockery.

"You know what else my ma used to say?" he said, leaning back in.

"No, I don't, 'cause she wasn't my ma."

"Ha. Well, Miss Smart-Ass. She used to say a hard head make a soft behind." He squeezed her hip, and she could feel him hardening as his eyes softened. She leaned her face into his. The dog shifted his weight underneath the couple, but he did not leave.

The three of them sat on the porch watching the sunlight

fade and the faint moon darken against the deepening sky. The familiar sounds from the woods surrounded them with their night calls, a sound that Mary found deeply satisfying and Burt regarded as an urgent message. One that screeched secrets and horrors, but he dared not spoil the evening with more of what Mary called crazy talk. He sat on the porch and let himself be warmed by his woman and his dog, by the earthiness of them.

Comfort was temporary, he knew. And believing in the longevity of a comfortable life for a man like him in a place like this—that was downright dangerous.

DELUSIONS

FOR THREE MONTHS after graduating college, I trudged around in a funk back at our house in DeRidder with Mama and my youngest siblings. The house was not the same without Grandmama and Papa, both of whom had died while I was away at college. Sleeping on a daybed in the den and waking to the sounds of my little brothers playing in the mornings was not the future I had envisioned for myself.

"Be patient—you'll find a job soon. Watch," Mama said.

Soon couldn't come soon enough.

In DeRidder, the pickings were slim. I may have written someone at the *Beauregard News* with a job inquiry, but I don't remember. The truth was, I didn't want to be home. I had left for college with visions of loft living in a city.

I worked as a substitute teacher for a bit and then drove out to Georgia to stay with Dena, her husband, and my young nephew. I worked a few temp jobs while applying to newspapers around the state.

In my fourth month of underemployment, one of the city desk editors at the newspaper in northern Louisiana where I had done my college internship tracked me down.

"What have you been doing since graduation?" he asked me.

"Traveling, studying, honing my skills," I said, trying to sound professional.

"We liked the work that you did for us when you were here as an intern," he said. "We'd like to offer you a full-time staff reporter job. How does that sound?"

It sounded like I was on my way.

"What do you think you can most contribute to the paper?"

"I know that I will be under a lot of deadline pressure, but I also look forward to spending some time, when I can, researching and flushing out longer stories."

"Fleshing out?"

I laughed sharply. "Oh, yes."

"Good. We don't want you flushing stories around here." He was bemused.

I hung up the phone, horrified.

My new career's hours were long, but the ground for me to grow professionally proved fertile. My editors assigned me to a variety of issues—education was my favorite—and asked me to pen a bimonthly column about community and national topics.

I had less than two years under my belt when the New Orleans paper called me for an interview. An older cousin, who had been a photojournalist at the paper, had recommended me for consideration. I was still as green as a grasshopper. The three-day interview landed me my first airplane ride. The commuter plane chopped violently across the skies separating Monroe from New Orleans—that "den of iniquity" as one acquaintance described it.

I didn't view New Orleans that way at all. Having studied French since second grade, I dreamed of Paris, Avignon, and New Orleans of old. The fact that New Orleans offered a melding of African, French, and Spanish cultures fascinated me. On the cab ride from the airport, I might as well have been visiting another country.

"What brings you to town?" the driver, an elderly black man, asked me.

"I have an interview at the daily newspaper here."

"The *Times-Picayune?*"

I nodded proudly.

"That rag of a paper? You do know what *picayune* means, don't you?" His eyes searched mine in the rearview mirror. He snorted at my silence.

"Not even a penny's worth!" he said. "That's what it means. Now, who in their right mind would go and name their paper something like that, then charge an arm and a leg for it all these years later? I don't like the way they cover my city. No siree."

"Well, I will do my part to fix some of that," I said naively.

The cab driver was wrong, I decided as I met with editors and reporters who wined and dined me in eclectic restaurants. They all seemed so worldly and liberal, the epitome of progressive ideals and intellect. I envisioned linking forces with them in a mission to expose and change the ills that stymied the people who lived in the city I was already falling hard for and to celebrate its—and its people's—beauty.

I landed the job, but soon discovered that my change-making powers were close to nil. The editors assigned me to a satellite office in a nearby town called Chalmette, a place once known as KKK territory. It was one of New Orleans's rejects. To be sent to this office meant you were at the bottom of the totem pole, for sure, and I would find racial embers smoldering in and around the town—from confederate symbols to a city council member using the word "nigger rigged" during a meeting to make his point about a piece of proposed legislation he didn't like.

My apartment was situated on the rim of New Orleans, in New Orleans East, populated by mostly black residents and bearing none of the architectural and historical richness that one associates with the city. I wanted to be in the center of New Orleans, where my big-dog colleagues worked in the paper's headquarters. I wanted to rent an old house with striking wood floors, not a carpeted modern template. But the proximity of my place to my office was what had drawn me to the New Orleans East suburb. I worked long hours and returned to the giant apartment building and into my oversized, sparsely furnished unit, feeling light-years away from the New Orleans the paper had shown me during our courting phase.

WHEN RIC AND his brothers were still boys, their mother warned them, "Y'all better marry white women. Black women will drag you down." In many ways, I have wondered if she had really been talking about herself.

A childhood memory that Ric has never forgotten stretches back to a day when he was with his siblings, mother, and one of her girlfriends at a park in Harlem, sitting on a blanket. They were enjoying ice cream cones from the Softee Ice Cream truck that stood just a few feet away blaring its signature musical chimes.

Ric's mother went to reach into her purse—perhaps for an extra napkin—but she stopped and handed Ric her cone before she dug her hand into the purse. Delicately, little Ricky grabbed her cone with his napkin so that his fingers would not touch it.

His mother's girlfriend jokingly said to him, "Take a lick."

Bernice turned to her and said, "He'd better not put his pussy lips on my ice cream."

Years later, I would stare at a photo of Ric's eight-year-old self and make myself sick with yearning, wishing I could reach back in time to hold him, to wipe the sadness from his long puppy-dog eyes, and to tell him it was okay to smile.

He rarely smiled, perhaps because he didn't trust his lips. He didn't trust his lips because his mother had hated the shape of them; she had called the lips of the child she pushed out of her own vagina pussy lips, as if that were some nasty and shameful thing.

I imagine him standing under her hateful spews, trying to hold in his lips, except it never worked because that thing— pussy lips—was powerful. It would detach itself from his face and creepy crawl its way down his chin to his neck and the rest of his body and then back up again to slither inside the hole that it had left on his face, working its way down to his feet, which became heavy things sticking to the floor until that's what his whole body felt like from the inside out: something indecent, something that should be hidden, something squishy and sticky and smelly, even though that something was responsible for his very existence.

He must have begun to hate this thing, that is to say, to hate himself, who was somehow one thing yet two: lips. These things that had stretched apart so that his infant head could emerge into a world where daddies left you and mamas called you the thing they most hated about themselves, leaving you to both flee toward and away from the others who either wanted to castrate or study or objectify you.

Black women will drag you down.

Ric had nearly escaped this fate until he met and some-how agreed to marry me on the cusp of his fortieth birthday. Although I was the one who had encouraged Ric to take me to New York to meet his mother, and though I helped soften the decades-old uneasiness between them by laughing, by teasing them both, by flattering his mother until she blushed, I blamed her for that hard place in him that would not—could not—melt completely.

When her youngest son grew up to date only white or Asian women, she complained bitterly.

"Son, aren't you ever interested in a woman who looks like me?"

But she was the one who planted the seed: White is better. Anything is better than black.

RIC AND I wrote our own vows. We hired a local black jeweler to create matching wedding bands. The jeweler carved the ankh symbol in the middle of each thick gold band. Neither Ric nor I had yet stepped foot in the motherland, but we grabbed the lowest-hanging symbol we knew to connect us to the land of our imagination.

My friend Vera made us a broom to match my wedding dress. As though she were bundling a baby, she wrapped the broom in raffia and wound burgundy-wine and antique-gold fabric, ribbons, and dried flowers throughout. She added a living thing: baby's breath.

We picked out the perfect place, one of historical and emotional meaning: Congo Square in Louis Armstrong Park, located in historically black Faubourg Treme. In the 1700s and 1800s, enslaved Africans had gathered there to dance, sing, trade, and breathe on Sundays, a day that French rulers had declared a nonworkday, even for the very people they worked to the bone. Before the Africans, the area was sacred ground to the Houmas Indians, who celebrated their annual corn harvest there.

I tried to imagine these ancestors. I felt little chills roll up my arms, confirmation that we were doing the right thing.

We would jump the broom there, on the soil of African ancestors who jumped the broom to signify their union since they were not legally allowed to marry. We would marry legally and be humbled by the indignities those before us faced.

We hired a black woman to officiate, a judge who was a mentor to two of our attorney friends, a couple who served as our official witnesses. A few days before our wedding day, a group of friends joined me to choose an area at Congo Square to have the wedding. We did not seek the city's permit. There was no time for red tape and rules. We would simply rise early and join friends under my special tree.

"This is it," I said, walking away from the cobbled cement that makes up the designated Congo Square area. I pointed to a live oak tree that seemed to sit apart from the others, tall and broad and sure. "I want to have our feet planted on the dirt here when we marry," I explained. "This is the one."

A MONTH AFTER Ric and I married, I quit my job at the newspaper. Being part of a writers' workshop had emboldened my dreams of writing full-time from home and enrolling in an MFA program.

Ric and I had been talking about moving on from the paper for more than a year. We bonded over our evening critiques of the microaggressions of some of our colleagues and editors and the frustration with not being able to dive into the stories we wanted to cover, especially those impacting New Orleans's overwhelmingly black population—stories that captured people's full humanity, not just crime reports and photos of musicians entertaining in the French Quarter.

Ric's work satisfaction was at least higher than mine. He was able to peruse the streets and alleys in New Orleans in between assignments, looking for interesting angles that he sometimes pitched to his editors and at other times pursued on his own. Because I was stuck in a satellite bureau, covering the people and happenings in New Orleans proper wasn't part of my jurisdiction.

The paper paid well, and our cost of living was low, so I doubled up on savings and started making contacts at other local publications to weave together a steady freelance stream. My income would be a small fraction of what it was; nevertheless, I had Ric's blessings. My leaving, he said, would help him get his butt into gear to start looking for another job. Although I had once sworn never to leave New Orleans, I had to accept that Ric's next move would likely take us to a larger paper, magazine, or agency out of state—or out of the country.

At home, my favorite way to unwind was listening to Nina Simone or Billie Holiday. Ric introduced me to Curtis Mayfield and Gil Scott-Heron, and their lyrics kept the embers of self-realization burning as we read books that included Nathan McCall's *Makes Me Wanna Holler* and Jill Nelson's *Volunteer Slavery*, both of which examine discriminatory practices in the newsroom.

My working relationship with my second newspaper editor, a micromanaging man in his late thirties or early forties, was strained. Larry might have resented the fact that his higher-ups had moved me from the St. Bernard Parish bureau to his satellite office in Metairie after I spoke with one of them about the difficulty of covering such a segregated community. Larry was leery of me and likely thought I was not experienced enough to be in his larger bureau, which dealt heavily with political stories.

My interests were, indeed, more lifestyle oriented; I was not as captivated by reporting, for instance, on a new education policy as I was in going inside a classroom, inside a teacher's head, or inside a family's home to see how that policy would eventually affect their realities. I ran out to cover house fires and car accidents because I had to, but I was more fascinated with the effects that the aftermath of these incidents had on my subjects. I was drawn to story and wanted to bring reports to life, and I wanted time and space to do that.

I desperately needed a mentor.

Instead, I had yet another editor to whom I could not relate, who was just tolerating me as he watched me like a hawk, sneaking up at my desk to peer at my screen before belting out, "Boo!"

"The next time he does that crap, turn around and ask him if he needs you to give him a white sheet," said my friend Patricia, a Costa Rican woman who worked in the advertising department.

"As in a white sheet for a ghost or the KKK?"

"Both!"

We laughed and laughed, and I could not wait for the opportunity.

"He doesn't think I belong here. I can feel it. He doesn't assign interesting stories to me. He doesn't encourage my ideas in meetings. He just sticks up his nose and makes condescending comments and snorts. Really, he's a child."

"He's a jackass, I can tell," Patricia said. "He doesn't like when I come over to talk to you. It's all over his face."

The next time I felt Larry creeping up on my cubicle, little flurries of giddiness and fury fluttered in my abdomen.

"Boo!" he said.

My fingers stopped typing. I let them hover above my keyboard. I turned my head slightly to the left, my eyes meeting Larry's tie—a navy-blue-and-gray strip of generic blah—and then lifted my head slowly, slowly, until my nose was high in the air, and I was somehow looking down on Larry even as he towered above me.

"Boo?" My tone was full of scorn. "But—where is your white sheet?"

Larry's eyes widened. He turned away sharply, covering his mouth in a short cough.

When he turned back to me, his eyes were cold. "What did you say?"

"You said 'boo,' so I'm asking you: Where is your white sheet? It is a ghost you're trying to be, right?"

Larry's face transformed into a ghoulish stretch of smile.

"Ah—Casper. Yes. Booooooo," he said, chuckling and walking away.

"Yeah, right. Casper."

I submitted my two weeks' notice a few months later, thanking my hiring editors and the publisher for the opportunity to work at the paper. Almost certain they would not care, I wrote, nevertheless, of my plans for my future: to enroll in grad school, freelance, and pen creative works. After I left, the paper ran one last piece I wrote—an essay that I had written in my writing workshop. But my career in the full-time newspaper world was over, and I would soon be an apparition, barely leaving an imprint on the craft or the community, barely allowing it to mold me.

DISTANCE

TO BE IN an intimate relationship with a photojournalist is to acquire a catalog of your life. You wonder if he is using his camera lens to see you more clearly—and therefore, love you more certainly—or if you are just the subject of the moment, a thing to be composed and lit and exposed.

His catalog of images of you becomes an interesting thing: it presents you with views of yourself in all your incarnations, and you hope you are as lovely as the attractive ones suggest and not as much of a mess as the ones you'd like to burn.

Ric aimed his lens at me countless times, but I never felt completely free to trust what it would capture. If I was not sleeping or facing another direction or partially eclipsed by someone else, I squirmed.

One night, as I sat working at my desk in the foyer, Ric was busy in his office, scanning negatives into his computer, toning them, and printing the keepers on sheets of matte paper. I heard him laughing at one point but chose to ignore him.

A few minutes later, his footsteps moved toward me.

"Guess who?" he said, sliding a print onto my keyboard.

I jumped up.

"Ric! Oh no, oh no!"

I looked at the photograph. It was a full-color, eight-by-ten-inch image of me naked. In the photograph, I am looking in the direction of the camera, clearly, but appear to be completely unaware of my nakedness, my vulnerability. I seem confident, as if I didn't think I'd ever be staring at this vision of myself. Judging by the length of my hair, Ric must have taken the photograph over a year earlier.

"Why are you processing this now? Why at all?"

In the photograph, I am dancing, but it looks as if I am in a warrior pose; my right arm raised to form a V and my hair and facial expressions wild.

I ignored this show of strength and pointed out my flaws.

I should have held in my lower abs; I should have run a comb through my hair (it was in an Afro), I should have wiped the oily sheen from my face and softened my expression.

"If you ever show this to anyone, I'll have to hurt you," I said.

"But look," Ric pointed out, "at the way the light is hitting your skin and the polished wood floor." He was proud of his work. That is what photographers do: immortalize moments in our lives whether we approve of what is in the frame or not. The camera catches some sliver of truth, raw and unguarded, freezing it. In the absence of images, we are inclined to remember inaccurately or fabricate entirely.

Both attracted to and repelled by the image of me, I leaned in and examined this version of myself, studying contours and varying shades, the inward curve of the spine, the deeply bent arches of feet, the wide diamond-shaped face, the pinkish-brown pucker of mouth, the white marbles of large eyes, and the black pupils swimming in the middle of all that white.

IN A DREAM, I get off the subway in New York City. It is raining. The rain, light and soft, massages my head.

I walk the streets, looking for a restaurant called Red Fish Grill. I find the restaurant, housed in a wooden cottage in a residential neighborhood. I look through the windows. It is dark inside. White-cloth covered tables are spaced across the floor in diamond-shaped patterns. Wine glasses are turned down. I try the door. It gives, and I walk inside.

A white man, a young maître d', has entered just before me. I worry about dripping rain on the restaurant's beautiful polished wooden floors. The maître d' doesn't seem to notice. He tells me that the restaurant is about to launch an exhibit on American lynchings. He says the restaurant is going to do something special with the long white tablecloths, something unique and dramatic. They are going to hang them from the ceiling to mirror the mood of the exhibit.

"My great-grandfather was lynched," I blurt out as I remove my boots to let them dry.

"Oh. Not a good thing," the man says casually, dismissively, and then turns to the door, back to his exhibit.

"No," I call after him. "Not a good thing at all."

But I am talking to myself.

TWO YEARS AFTER we married in 2001, Ric and I left behind our family and friends and all that we loved in New Orleans in search of new opportunities. New Orleans had been, for me, the perfect blend of cosmopolitan, historic preservation, mystery, and art, but both Ric and I had our sights set on expanding our careers. Our feathers, we believed, were made of the same stuff: we were two black storytellers, one visual and one print, one northern and one southern, who had converged in New Orleans and were now following the flocks of black Louisianans who had, during Jim Crow, moved to California in search of better lives—in search of saving their lives.

We sold or gave away most of our furniture, bringing mostly books, clothing, and our dreams from the city of saints to the city of angels. Cities get cloaked in their nicknames and in our collective dreams for them, as children do in their parents' dreams and names for them. Sometimes they reflect back the best of what we dreamed up for them; at other times, they are the preacher's kid: rebellious and full of scorn. The best a parent, or a city dweller, can do is ride the storms and the calm with patience, with grace.

Ric aimed to advance his photojournalism career at the Associated Press's downtown Los Angeles office. I enrolled in grad school in Marina del Rey; my days were filled with reading, writing, discussing books with fellow students, and, for a little while, selling antiquarian books to put a few dollars in the bank. After my savings from New Orleans ran out, Ric was the main breadwinner, and I was overcome with feelings of failure and guilt.

Our apartment was in Glendale, a suburb northeast of downtown LA. Using an online apartment hunter, I had chosen the place while still in New Orleans. I wanted it to feel as much like New Orleans as possible. Los Angeles listens to what its transplants say we want; it listens to our dreams of the future weighed down by yearnings for the past and teases us with replicas of those yearnings. But on its own terms.

Our new apartment lacked the high ceilings of the double-shotgun houses we had rented in New Orleans, but it was nestled inside a small 1920s Spanish stucco building and had old French windows, curio cabinets, and wood floors that I let breathe instead of covering over with rugs.

Owners of a few books on feng shui, we prided ourselves on being minimalists. I thought the practice aligned with Ric's White Crane Kung Fu philosophies: providing a clean and deceptively simple form, being at one with nature, and maintaining attention to detail and balance. The walls were a soft white that we never got around to painting, despite my desire to see them come alive with color. The décor was a hodgepodge of our childhood relics, as well as art I had picked up from the New Orleans Jazz Fest, Community Book Center, and French Quarter vendors.

I hung an arched mirror inside the entryway to echo the arch that led into the greater room. I also hung two of our childhood photographs there, which were set in a bamboo-green wooden frame designed to look like an old window panel. I liked to stop and look at us: the spicy-looking toddler I had been and the little brown-faced boy with a sad, crooked smile and big wistful eyes that Ric had been.

Ric and I slept in the living room on a futon that I covered in printed textiles. With this arrangement, he was able to use the bedroom as an office and darkroom. My office sat off the kitchen, taking over what would have been the breakfast nook. I kept the French windows open to welcome the breezes and the scents that wafted in from my elderly Armenian neighbors' kitchens. The breakfast nook was surrounded by built-in book-cases and crannies. In one scalloped cutout, I displayed the decorative broom that Vera had made for our wedding.

A woods-inspired or nag champa incense was always burning in our home, with its trail of smoke mingling with the scent of curried lentils or black beans simmering on the stove.

We were a couple who had pledged allegiance to our goals as artists. In one of Ric's snapshots, I am standing, bent at the waist, over my laptop with my right fingers on the keyboard and my left fingers pressed against my mouth. It is a profile shot. Unaware of him standing there with the camera, I am engrossed in my work. It is evident that I don't have my contacts in because of the way I am squinting at the screen. My desk is littered with notes, highlighters, and my eyeglasses. Taped to the wall above the desk are handwritten pages that I had undoubtedly planned to work into the story that I was just beginning to try to piece together about my family.

I didn't know where I was going with the story, but I knew I wanted to start with Burt Bridges, with what I had heard about him. He was an invisible part of my identity, and there was something about being in a city as massive as Los Angeles that made me want to unearth all the hidden parts of me. In this unearthing, surely there would be an anchor, something to grab onto in this city of ocean waves and ground that shakes. In my quest then, I was looking to understand, and therefore save, myself. I could not see that my future would stretch beyond my own body, mind, and work.

Looking back, though, there were urges that I had planted unknowingly. In our living room, a fertility doll stood on top of the stereo. Nearby, a wrought-iron side table was adorned with a plant and the carved image of a pregnant woman carrying a basket over her head. Her breasts were free and her stomach curved with child.

Neither of us, two people who had decided not to have children, thought to question why we had such images of fertility in our home.

I LOVE SOUTHERN CALIFORNIA—Mount Wilson, the shops and restaurants, the open markets, the endless variety of people, and every imaginable thing. When I stand at the mouth of the Pacific Ocean, I think of the Atlantic and how it is a similar color early in the morning, gray-blue, before it turns vacation green. I think of our ancestors, of how we came here through them, all of us. A cloud becomes a ship and another a scroll. The ocean roars, complains, and bears witness. It washes up memories of bodies and drowns my standing feet.

When I climb to the top of Griffith Park, I feel a shifting inside me like the earth's plates underneath my feet. I imagine myself as a hill of salt, wondering if an earthquake or strong Santa Ana wind will soon send me flying back to the mud of my youth.

During our first year in Los Angeles, we basked in sunlight and shared moments of discovery hunting down great vegetarian and vegan restaurants across the county, driving down the 101 with the top down on the sports car Ric bought, meeting interesting new friends and breaking bread with them at dinner parties, and trudging across the sand at beaches to work our calf muscles deeper when we exercised together. Mostly, though, our time was spent apart. The days stretched before me. Evenings and weekends also challenged my notions of marriage, as Ric's passion for Kung Fu came in second place to his photography. When he put down his camera, he picked up his saber.

As I worked in my master's program, he took care of me financially, made sure my car was maintained, and encouraged me to finish my degree and not worry about making money for the moment.

But I wanted touch, time, and tenderness.

"You treat me like your little sister," I complained. "I don't want to be your little sister; I want to be your wife."

But surrounded by this mass of asphalt, he seemed to grow harder, colder. He was angry and frustrated by what he viewed as a stifling work environment. He seethed over the frivolity of his photo assignments at the wire service. His editors had promised he would have a chance to carve out a different kind of role for himself, continuing his characteristic theme of documenting the "resiliency of the human spirit" in the face of despair and disaster. Instead, they assigned him to spend his hours chasing Lakers' games and brush fires, as well as photographing Hollywood stars (in flesh, in wax, in cement). He needed to tell real stories, he said, and so in his spare time, Ric went digging for those societal issues most of us keep swept away in the corners of our minds. On self-funded projects, he documented poverty and sickness in Los Angeles, Vietnam, and South Africa. I understood, for I was almost as passionate about his career as he was and so completely proud of him, this black man who told stories about the plight of disempowered people.

I wished there were a way he could do both: be a hero with his camera and with his wife.

A SMALL PARK, shaped like a horseshoe, sat across the street from our apartment. One evening, I walked over to the park to write; my newly forming dreadlocks hung over my forehead like vines.

An hour later, an Armenian woman, short and humped, settled down next to me on the splintered, gray wooden bench. She was dressed in long, thick, black garments; black socks; and black leather sandals. The sun was, as usual, baking—even on its way down; still, the woman, draped in all those clothes, did not fan herself. Her skin was dry. Her soft gray curls were wrapped loosely in a flowered orange satin scarf. The skin on her legs—slivers of it visible between her socks and the bottom of her slightly ruffled skirt—folded in shiny olive wrinkles.

She pointed to my pages.

"English?" she asked, then said something else in Armenian. I shrugged my shoulders and offered a stupid, apologetic smile.

She became frustrated. "Humph."

With her small hand, she waved away my attempts to explain that I do not speak her language. She dabbed a tissue at her eyes and then brushed invisible lint from her black coat. She stood up and spread a part of her newspaper on the bench before sitting down again. I pretended to return to writing. A tiny black speck of a bug rolled across my page.

The woman turned to the rest of her newspaper, written in figures that looked, to me, a bit like intricate curls on a wrought-iron gate in the French Quarter. After she skimmed for a few moments, she rolled the tabloid up like a scroll. She stood up to leave and snapped her fingers for my attention. I mistakenly believed she was telling me goodbye, and I smiled, but she grabbed my arm and pointed to another set of benches, over yonder, inside a circle of cement. She jerked her head in the direction of two elderly Armenian men who were dressed neatly in their navy-blue and charcoal suits. I surmised that they came to the park every evening around this time and that we were sitting on their bench. The woman's fingers dug into my arm with urgency.

"Okay," I said, amused. I pressed my notebook to my chest; grabbed my keys, pens, and book; and followed her.

She did not let go of my arm until we were seated in our new spot. She looked at the men, giggled like a girl, and then threw back her head for a full laugh. I laughed, too, heartily, even though I didn't know why we were laughing. Eventually, though, our laughter met at a crossroads of comprehension, and I realized that it was not just the trip to the park that sustained the men and defined their evening ritual; it was also the day-after-day process of descending on the same bench—that anchor of familiarity. We surrendered the bench to them because their world would be turned upside down without it. Oh, let them have their aging, splintered throne, the woman's laughter murmured to mine. Let them have that.

Our new bench was metal; its cold iron arms were between us, but we were linked in a warm, invisible embrace. Another stooped Armenian woman came to sit on the other side of me. She was wearing an olive-green shirtdress that looked like it came from a 1980s Sears Roebuck catalog. She sat with one hand folded over her stomach and the other cupping her chin. Every now and then she let out a heavy sigh. Over her sighs, or underneath them, I heard the leaves whistling in the wind like mild chimes, the birds singing their final choruses of the evening, and the men's shoes pushing softly against the grass.

When Ric and I moved to the neighborhood, the first thing I noticed was how absent it was of the young brown bodies that crowded our neighborhood streets in New Orleans. Our new neighborhood was predominantly Armenian, most of them elderly, and some mornings, when I would glance up from my computer and look out the window, I found myself being watched by one or two of the women who stood on the second-floor balcony of the apartment across from mine, squinting down at me. They averted their gaze when I raised my face to them. Clad in their sweaters and housedresses, they reminded me of my grandmother and her elderly friends—Miss Christine, Sister Ruby, and Miss Emma Dee—on Elm Street.

One day, I saw a van parked in front of an Armenian restaurant. The date, April 24, 2002, and the slogan, WE WILL NEVER FORGET, were painted in bright gold letters against the black van, announcing the eighty-seventh anniversary of the Armenian genocide. Reportedly, the Ottoman Empire massacred about 1.5 million Armenians. I learned that the Turkish government denied the genocide, as though the starvations, killings, and forced exiles were merely apparitions of the Armenians' imaginations.

I was ignorant of this history before we moved to Glendale. As I sat with the women on the bench that day, I wanted to talk to them about their home country and about my family's past, where horror and denial also coexisted.

Since language eluded us, I focused instead on the wind, our silence, and the heavy scent of cumin and garlic drifting from kitchen windows. I leaned deeply into the bench and wrote. The sun was almost gone when I looked up again, but the women were still beside me.

We were a three-headed shadow against the cemented ground.

IN MY MFA PROGRAM, a new writer friend, a Filipino American man, tried to sway me to change directions with my story.

"Here you are, yet another black writer writing about race," he said one evening after we had shared our stories in progress in a workshop. "Haven't so many others already written about race? About black and white?"

"What do you mean?" I asked, bristling.

He pressed on, undeterred—determined, in fact, to make his point to get me to stop. "I'm just saying it would be cool, different, interesting, if the black writer did not write about race, at least, not in black-and-white terms."

"But you write about gay issues, and you're gay," I argued. "Isn't that typical?"

He tried another tactic. "But you are so funny. I mean, really funny, yet that's not in your work. You should write out that funny side of you. We've got to make ourselves fully expressed in our stories."

He elbowed me and grinned. I didn't reciprocate.

Usually I am laughing. There are pictures of me with my mouth stretched wide open—as though by an invisible clamp—in rapturous laughter, the kind that hurts real good.

In my stash of childhood photographs, there is no documentation of this openmouthed laughter, although I am sure I laughed, despite often being somber then. No, my laughs were not captured on film until I was in college. I look at those photos, one after the other, of me with my mouth wide open in laughter, and the memories erupt.

Like the memory of me drunk, belly flat on a bridge on my college campus. My friends and I had mixed gin and Cisco, orange-flavored, and drank glass after glass.

"I'm swimming. I'm swimming," I said while lying on the

sidewalk leading back to our dorm. My words scratched past the laughter in my throat like skin skidding on concrete. My legs and arms flapped. I jumped up from the concrete. "I'm the Road Runner," I said, and took off running and laughing—with my friends hooting with laughter behind me.

Another memory: I am laughing, laughing, laughing, and the kids at DeRidder High School make fun of my cackles.

"There goes the hyena again," they said.

My algebra teacher separated me from my friends, placing me on the other side of the room.

"This isn't stand-up hour," she reprimanded. "And your voice, Miss Sandy, carries."

My crabby high school French teacher despised me for my laugh because she believed I was laughing at her.

My adult friends love my laugh, gravitate toward it, bask in it like kids around a campfire listening to ghost stories. My laugh is like hot marshmallows melting on the tongue.

"Your laugh is contagious," they say, one after another.

"I would know your laugh anywhere," another friend once said.

At a restaurant one night, Ric said something funny in his dry way. I fell over my plate, laughing and laughing, but his expression remained unmoved because, well, that is how he is. The other diners looked at me suspiciously. Is she drunk? High?

"I want you in my audience whenever I do get the nerve to get on the stand-up stage," a friend had said.

I felt my laughter bubbling up, giggles that tickled and scratched the wet skin of my throat and shot out past my teeth. Quickly, before the second wave, I covered my full-lipped mouth with my right hand, an attempt to hide a gap on my right side that used to not be there. I covered also to muffle the volume of this laughter that is my body, but it shot out anyway and from all parts of me—my neck, my elbows, my knees—until I was doubled over. Laughing. Laughing. A hyena. An orangutan. A windup toy. A centuries-old howl.

ANOTHER NEW CALIFORNIA writer friend—petite and blond, with skin nearly as white as milk—appeared distressed after she heard me give a reading of my reimagined story of Burt's lynching.

After the reading, she approached me. A dark pink painted her cheeks as she said, "I don't want to believe stuff like that happened and to the family members of people I know." She shook her head. "No. I can't believe this. I have family in the South."

She stared at me, waiting, and I wondered if it were accusation or disbelief or shame emanating from her eyes. I couldn't be sure, so I did not know how to answer. I shifted the bulk of my weight from my right leg to my left. I had thought it might be safe to revisit such a story out here in California, where museums of tolerance and history also dredge up sleeping dogs from other eras.

How could I tell her that while I enjoyed our breezy beach days, I have always been drawn to what is sad and to what is heavy?

Born at the hands of a midwife named Miss Shade, on a street named Shady Lane, I am used to that which is shrouded; my mind is structured around it, seeks it out. When I would shed my clothes and stretch my naked brown body, back flat, in an empty tub and lie as still as a corpse, watching evening darken the window, what was I inviting? What child seeks—craves—darkness?

The same one who finds comfort in it as an adult: roaming graveyards and obsessing over the death of her ancestor. I watch the light from darkness's viewpoint. I retreat from the sun, pushing it to a corner of my memory; it is a dim disk so many worlds away.

My friend was still watching me, and she was still waiting.

"Yes, it did happen," I said. "I don't know the details, but, yes, it happened." I was tempted to say I'm sorry, but that would sound ridiculous. Besides, I had sat down and written this story. I had wanted to write it. For what would I apologize?

I could have made light of it all after I finished reading to try to get everybody to laugh. I could have said, "Hey, y'all, that was a bad family joke that my folks have been passing around for a century. You know, like a ghost story. We're crazy like that."

Other people in the audience—some of them white poets and writers—urged me to keep going with my story.

"You must write this story," another new writer friend, Kaaren, who refuses to shed her sixties hippie soul, said. "You must. Just keep going."

But I had no idea where I was headed or what I would do once I got there.

FATIGUE SPELLS DOGGED me and worsened during our first couple of years in California. I visited five doctors to get to the root of my fatigue. Finally, a black woman doctor who was comprehensive, confident, and preparing for early retirement so that she could write children's books, discovered the cause: chronic Epstein-Barr virus.

I read as much as I could on the virus, but what stopped me in my tracks was a description by Dr. Jesse Stoff, coauthor of *Chronic Fatigue Syndrome: The Hidden Epidemic*:

> The Epstein-Barr Virus is unimaginably minute. Because the virus is actually smaller than the wavelength of light, it lives in a world without color; everything is black and white. And

yet it displays extraordinary detail, geometrically complex and perfect, like a Herkimer diamond.

Medical researchers say that at least 90 percent of Americans are carrying some degree of the virus.

I was stunned by this poetics of biology. In those early days of illness, I used it as a metaphor to link what ailed me to a past—and present—constructed around concepts of black and white. We were, all of us, carrying inside us our country's sickness. But science—knowledge—couldn't save me or my attempts to create a better life; I could not save myself.

I finished my master's program in two years. Six months later, I landed a teaching job at a school for teens charged with everything from meth and marijuana use to gangbanging to rape. Together, we read and explored *Macbeth*, Curtis Mayfield's song "We People Who Are Darker Than Blue," *A Raisin in the Sun*, and *Julius Caesar*. I went to the kids' football and basketball games. I judged Ric harshly for not attending with me. But he was not interested in this new part of me that I had found with the teens. Perhaps he viewed it as a distraction from my purpose in moving to Los Angeles: to finish school and write. Still, I had to make money somehow, and teaching what I was passionate about was, I thought, an honorable compromise.

Every year around our wedding anniversary, Ric and I found ourselves entangled in some argument that started small, grew teeth, and led to us threatening to go our separate ways.

We would come back together again, talk things out, and try to move on, but an unsettledness was always at our backs, waiting—expectant.

MARY, 1904

MARY DOESN'T KNOW what Burt's last words were. She doesn't know whether the last name on his lips was hers or his mother's or his unborn son's. She doesn't know if he cried out against the pain of the rope against his neck, or tried to argue his case, or listed the qualities that he thought might have made his life seem more than worthwhile—precious.

He had defended himself against a man trying to hurt him, but he had not killed that man. He had not maimed him for life. He lost his life for fighting to live.

He could have explained all of this to the sheriff and his mob, but for what? They knew the real truth. What made them so hard and ugly? Mary wonders about that. The expression on her young face is already mirroring the meaning of her name: bitter, sea of sorrow. What mother would name her child such a terrible and sad name? But her mother had meant her no harm. Mary tries now to remember her face, but she can only recall the faces of the weeping and and wailing women at her mother's funeral. The sisters at the church found humility in sorrow.

"Give it all to God," they said.

But to Mary, those buckets of sorrow held water that wasn't hers. And the women's teachings seemed to let the white folks off free.

"Why we always the ones weeping and toting all the pain?" she says to herself.

The white folks she knows have never said a word about wailing through the night to repent on behalf of themselves and their community, on behalf of the world. The brutes who killed Burt had never taken a long hard look at themselves in the mirror; they didn't feel even a molehill of guilt. At the same time, despite their privilege of being able to walk around in the world free as birds, they weren't filled with an appreciation for life either. They didn't walk around appreciating the beauty and the turn of light the way Burt did, had never tuned their ears to any higher frequencies—the flutter of a hummingbird or dragonfly, say, or God's voice.

Did they know that whenever Burt had time, he planted flowers just to make Mary happy? Did they know he caught butterflies just to sense the joy in their quivering wings as he let them go? The men would not have cared about any of these small beauties about Burt. Watching him get joy out of something so simple would have broken open their simmering fury. The nigger had the nerve to own a store and think he was better than them. Who the hell did he think he was? Not their equal, not white, not sacred, not even human.

To silence the questions darting in her mind, Mary settles on this: As proud and as daring as he was, Burt did not have any last words. His cries, poetic and pleading, would have multiplied the stones in their hearts, shattering any sliver of mercy they may have thought, for a blink, to conjure. They were one heavy rope of no mercy.

Mary is crying, but the tears rain down on the inside of her, where no one can see. She unfastens the front of her dress and picks up her baby to nurse him. She clamps down on a whimper at the first pang on her nipple, refusing even to allow herself to acknowledge this physical pain. She will not let Houston see her mourning his daddy. Burt would not want that.

STORMS

I SAW A tornado once, although I do not know what part is my memory and what part is the memory of my mother's retelling of the storm.

It sounded like the whistling and rumbling of a dozen trains speeding along rusted tracks, like warring choruses of clashing brass cymbals and roars of thunder upon thunder, like angels and chariots and demons descending upon the earth.

Four years old, I ran to the living room window of our little green house that sat alone in the midst of pine trees.

"Get away from that window!" Mama screamed.

But my brain was shutting down my body; it could not process what my eyes were absorbing. The source of the sound was the wind. What struck me was that this wind had a definite shape, and it was coming directly toward me. The things that clung to it—leaves, dirt, clothing—gave manifest to its form and its fury.

Mama yanked up my frozen body and, carrying me under one arm and Dena under the other, ran to the bathroom and placed us in the tub for safety. The tornado spun around our house in DeRidder, leaving it unscathed. It tore through other parts of the town, ripping off roofs and siding, lifting cars and vans and trees.

Our house survived, yet the real storm was inside of us; we

were a family being torn apart by marital strife. A little while after the tornado, Mama packed two trash bags, one filled with toys, the other with clothes, and left my father—his lies, his philandering, his hot hands—for good.

IN 2005, WHEN the waters from Hurricane Katrina destroyed inadequate levees, swallowing and spitting out the city my soul still craves, infidelity was slinging my own marriage against a rock, cracking it wide open, and leaving my hopes and dreams for a perfect romance, a perfect marriage, exposed and rotting.

From the dry safety of Southern California, I watched Katrina batter New Orleans as television cameras captured the war between water, wind, and man. And while people, possibly people I knew, were being washed away, I was absorbed in romantic drama.

Each time I tried to call my friends who still lived there, I was met with a busy signal or a recording that the lines were down.

I was overcome with guilt. In pursuit of new experiences, I felt that I had abandoned New Orleans, its people, its children, and the few friends who remained in the city, those who had not migrated to San Francisco, New York City, Pittsburgh, or Chicago. Why hadn't I called my old friends earlier with the first news of a possible evacuation? Like the day I stood at the window as the tornado rolled toward me, my senses were dulled, and I had been too slow to act.

A New Orleans friend who had moved to Pennsylvania phoned me, panic lining her voice. She had spoken to Harold, who was staying temporarily with friends and family in Los Angeles until the floods were over, but she had not been able to reach another friend, Vera.

"Sand, what are we going to do?" she asked.

I felt thrust into the role of big sister, a role I usually stepped into easily as the eldest of five. My friends—and siblings—always relied on me to have it together.

They relied on me to dole out uplifting advice.

They relied on me to be strong and successful in all things.

"I don't know, Tameka," I told her; my voice was weak and foggy. "I've been trying to reach her. I've called her son Dale but heard nothing. We have to just keep trying."

"Sand, are you okay?" she asked. "Harold told me you and Ric broke up. Oh my God, girl, I just can't believe it."

They relied on me to have and sustain the perfect marriage, and I had demolished all of that.

"Yes, Ric and I are getting a divorce."

"But why, Sand?" she asked.

Her why, full of curiosity and pain, swelled against the receiver, waiting, waiting, waiting for the truth.

Instead of delivering it—raw, ugly, vulnerable—I filled her ear with stock answers.

"It's for the best," I said, scrambling to comfort her and to camouflage my infidelity. "Ric and I are still best friends. We were just growing in different directions."

If I told her—them—the truth, they would never forgive me. How could they when I would never forgive myself?

"How are you holding up?" she asked.

"Oh, I'm fine. Really. But enough about me. We've got to find Vera. I can't even think about my own situation right now."

But thinking was all I had been doing. Not clear, measured thinking. It was the kind that bordered on fantasy and insanity. My conscience was eating me alive, and yet there I remained, entangled in an affair from which I believed I could not extricate myself. I was debris magnetized to a tornado.

ON A SATURDAY morning months into my affair, I told Ric the truth, or part of the truth.

Driven not by courage but by a foolhardy belief that true love awaited me on the other side of a marriage—two marriages—destroyed, I sat down on the side of the futon where Ric was oversleeping. He should have been up hours before because we had planned a short road trip in an effort to bring some spunk back into our marriage. He had suggested we drive up to one of the wineries, and I had cringed inwardly. As the hours ticked away that morning, I did not bother to wake him.

I watched him sleep. Finally, around ten, I wrapped my fingers around my husband's wrist. I felt the thin bones there and his pulse thrumming in his taut veins. With each pulse, I tried to find the perfect phrase to tell him that I had betrayed him; that this thing I was in had become all-consuming, swallowing my sanity, my love for him, and my loyalty to our marriage; that it would not, could not, let me go; and that I, too, clung to its intestines with delirium and desperation. I wanted to translate a painful beauty to Ric that would make what I had done justifiable instead of filthy. But the words turned to waste inside my mouth, and I lost the train of articulation as quickly as I lost his pulse with my concentration broken and my heart loud in my ears.

I shook him. "You overslept. It's after ten o'clock."

He pulled himself to his elbows, his eyes tired and red, his perfect locs framing cheeks that seemed even more sallow in the mornings.

"Why didn't you wake me?"

"I don't know. I don't know." I leaned toward him. "Ric, I don't know how to tell you . . ."

He yawned. "Tell me what?"

"That . . . that I've fallen in love with someone else." I held my breath, feeling unworthy of sharing the same oxygen he would need.

Ric sat up all the way. I could feel and see his chest closing in, hardening.

"Have you slept with him?"

I nodded.

"How many times?"

I drew my shoulders to my ears—a girl. "A couple of times."

I watched him watch the lie flicker in my eyes. He did not yell or look at me with disgust. He stared at me for a long while. When the questions came, they were icy and direct, forming a pyramid that did not linger long at the wide, bottomless base of why. He wanted the facts, hard and plain.

When I finished squeezing out the details I was willing to release (how I had met him, where we had sex, what his marital status was), Ric left for a long drive, crossing highways studded with strangers.

By nightfall, I was blaming Los Angeles—with its sprawling massiveness and arid air—for corroding the last vestiges of closeness Ric and I had shared in New Orleans, an environment that bred intimacy. I searched for justifications, although there is not always justice in justifications. In LA, hours that Ric and I could have spent together were separated by freeways and moving steel. The palm trees towered above us, impossibly distant compared to the moss-draped oak trees of the city I loved. We lived in an apartment that seemed out of place on a street filled with houses. In New Orleans, there was only one interstate; everything seemed connected, easily accessible. In that bowl-shaped city, everything felt circular: even when we were moving away from each other, there was already a feeling of coming back together. In the places I frequented when I was alone—the Whole Foods down the street from our house, Community Book Center, City Park, Bennachin Restaurant—people knew me as part of Ric and Sand.

"Where's your other half?" friends, waiters, grocery clerks

would ask. When we would come home from work, our neighbors would be outside, and they would greet us as we emerged from our cars.

WHEN RIC RETURNED from his drive that night, he was free—free of me, free of any nostalgia or conflict. There was no familiar warmth in his voice.

"I'm leaving." He looked at me, his head slightly tilted, revealing the sharp angles of his jawline. "I'm definitely leaving."

I was not surprised that he did not fight for me, for our marriage. I was, in the secret folds of myself, relieved.

"I love you, Sand," Ric said. "But I've been wishing I weren't married for the last year or so now."

I searched his words and his face for malice but found none. Everything had gone slack, flat. He seemed somewhat relieved as well.

"Why?" I asked. "How could you stay when you didn't want to be here?"

"I didn't know how to tell you because I do still love you, and I couldn't hurt you. I just couldn't do that to you."

His integrity and restraint stood in stark contrast to mine. They stood as a monument between us.

"Should we see a therapist?"

As the cliché slid to the floor, Ric stared at me.

Who are you? his eyes asked, yet with his mouth he said he had already begun to forgive me.

"The only thing I want in life right now, Sand, is to travel and tell stories. I don't want to be tied to anything."

By then, our lease was month to month. Ric decided we would put our intent-to-vacate notice in immediately. He helped me move into a quiet apartment building a few blocks from our old one. The two-story building was filled, mostly, with elderly Armenian couples and widows. My apartment, while a single, oddly included a kitchen big enough for a family, which depressed me beyond words. Once I was settled in, Ric moved to an apartment off bustling Hollywood Boulevard.

"I've hated living in the suburbs," he said.

But I had not known.

WEEKS LATER, the neglected levees collapsed, and the waters from Hurricane Katrina engulfed parts of New Orleans, smaller towns and little islands along the Mississippi and Gulf of Mexico. For weeks after that, the water was still receding. Dead bodies were still rising to the surface. Ric flew to New Orleans to cover the aftermath with his cameras. I was in California with its beautiful weather, closed up in my apartment where sunlight still broke through.

I curled myself in my bed at night and television images of New Orleans wavering in the water made my eyes well as I fell asleep. On one such evening, my missing friend, Vera, called. At fifty-five, she had been through more tribulations than I could imagine, and I wondered how she was going to fight her way through the aftermath of Katrina. Meanwhile, my self-pity made her testy.

"Sand, honey, like I used to tell you when you were running around here all naive: 'Life is a bitch, and then you die.' You gotta learn to just accept it and get over it."

My bed felt like a straitjacket—a casket made of wood panels painted the whitest of whites.

At the furniture store, the daybed had seemed so beautiful, dressed in a cream and cherry-colored down comforter and thick red-wine pillows, all of it sitting lusciously under a single shelf of books and a soft glowing light. In my apartment, the promise of the store display fell flat. The bed, backed against a stark white wall, proved too bulky for my small room.

On the other side of that wall lived a ninety-year-old woman who was ripe with dementia. As she hollered aloud at night, I released my own cries, confident her tormented screams drowned mine out. Our moans converged in the spaces between the wood and particleboard that separated us.

A COUPLE OF the Armenian women planted tomatoes for me in the planter outside my door. I saw their gesture as an act of welcome. Later, I read that the tomato (the "devil's apple") once symbolized evil, an association because of its toxic leaves. Were the women labeling me as toxic? Would the tomatoes, once they bloomed, stand tall like scarlet letters in front of my door, announcing to everyone the evil I had done to my husband, to another man's wife and child, to the institution of marriage? I thought back to my childhood when I was a tambourine-beating girl growing up in a fire-and-brimstone ministry.

What would Uncle Junior think of me now? As the senior pastor of our small church, Uncle Junior's yellowish-red eyes seemed full of judgment and omnipotence. I believed those eyes were capable of spewing flames from the lake of fire at any given moment.

As I jogged one morning, crushing fallen jacaranda leaves and passing bungalows and vans, visions of Mama, pregnant and alone and heartbroken, shut up in her room, flooded my memories. There must have been days when she did not want to go on. I know there were times she hated life. Growing up, I even felt there were times she hated me, us, her children: the products of a marriage and subsequent romances turned sour.

I wanted to call her—"Mama, help me. Mama, I need you"—but I could not. Despite all her romantic woes, she had always steered clear of married men and had been disgusted by the ones who pursued her.

"Nasty old thing," I heard her say once, and then, "His poor wife. Working hard like that, taking care of his children, and look how he thanks her."

No. I could not tell Mama what I—a wife—had done to another wife, another woman. Another family.

Mama could not save me, and I wasn't sure she would even want to. I had stood gazing out of the window of my own marriage and longing for something more. This time, I had called the storm to me, flung the door wide open, and invited it to come inside.

"YOU ARE WHAT I've been waiting for all my life," he said over and over again. With his eyes, with his words, with his tongue, his teeth, his thrusts, with his nose inhaling the scent of you before you were born and even into the future of you after you are gone, until there is no more of what he thought he needed of you left, and until he realized that what he was craving is not material and cannot be possessed or fucked to fulfillment.

The hole at the center of him is not pinpointable, will not go away, and so he exhaled, expelling you with this dawning. And whether it was after one night of loving or twenty years down the road, it doesn't matter: you are not his victim.

You, likewise, told him, "I've been waiting for you all my life," and you urged him to go deeper, deeper, deeper still, to fill you up with everything in him until you were both dizzy with that thing—captured love, lust, loneliness—and still it was not enough for the hungry creature inside of you. You, who were born waiting to feel your father's loving gaze upon your face, to feel the imprint of love in his palms as he cradled you, waiting for him to embrace the word *Daddy*, to not ignore you or frighten you or hate you.

And after your mother left him, you carried with you the emptiness of him, the memory of waiting for him at the front screen door of your grandparents' home because he promised; he promised this time he would come for real. It was Christmas, after all, and he had spent the week shopping for all kinds of toys and is headed to you and your sister with a load of toys in the bed of his white truck. You can almost see it: him and his white truck and the boxes of toys bobbing in the truck bed. You wait without whining because you have inherited patience or have learned it as a coping mechanism. You wait—from light to dark—until Grandmama tells you to come away from the door. Only then do the tears you tried so hard to hold back do what they wanted to do and fall anyway as you turn, bereft of a man who has become someone else's husband, someone else's father. A man who is fallible, who is certainly not God at all.

ECHOES

I DIDN'T KNOW until recently that Grandmama Avis and Papa Houston were both married before they met each other. Papa was fifteen; his wife was twelve. This girl, his wife, died of pneumonia, leaving him a widower before he graduated from his teens.

Grandmama, my mother reports, was around sixteen when she married her first husband. He ran off, and she never saw him again. Still, she lived in fear for many decades after that because the divorce papers never went through. *What if he's still out there?* she wondered, *and I'm married to two men?*

Near the end of Papa's life, he started to lose his memory and his recollections of these two women—the sickly girl and his wife of sixty-three years—began to play tricks with his mind. As his dementia worsened, there were days he completely forgot who Grandmama Avis was.

One day, she went in to care for him and he hollered at her, "Who are you?"

"Daddy," Grandmama Avis, said, a habit she'd started when their children were young, "I'm your wife." She said it quietly, waiting for recognition to dawn.

"You ain't none of my wife. My wife's name was Ana Mae and you ain't none of Ana Mae. You ain't none of my wife. Get out!"

Grandmama left the room and closed the door tight. She sat down and let sixty-three years of sobs flow from her.

"I'd never seen Mama cry like that unless she was burdened for someone under the power of the Holy Spirit," my mother recalled. "But never about herself. I had never heard that hurt kind of sound coming from her own heart."

At what point do all of our previous romantic relationships merge in our minds? When those earlier bodies with whom we were deeply intimate are physically disentangled from us, we still have their names, even when their faces and the scent of them fade.

Marcus called me Carol, the name of his ex-wife, twice. Once, during a tense argument where he stuttered to break through my diatribe to get his point across: "C . . . C . . . Carol . . ." And then another time, during a nightmare he was having, he yelled her name out into the dark while groping for me.

Carol changed her name shortly after their divorce, yet that is how he remembered her. Marcus, who was Marc Anthony Richardson, also went through the legal process of changing his name to rid himself of the last name that was the name of his brother's father, and changing his first name to a version that he thought better fit him.

But we can no more shed our original names than we can completely shed our souls of our previous partners. And I wonder if, way in the night or in the wee hours of the morning, John ever heard Mary whisper Burt's name. And I wonder how John could have thought that he could beat Burt out of Mary by beating her and her child.

He couldn't beat Burt Bridges out of Mary or Houston. Despite Mary's best intentions, that name still made it to my ears and will, I hope, continue to be echoed.

PART III

IDENTITY

A FEW WEEKS after I wrote the state of Louisiana, I received
a death certificate for Mary Buckley. But the death certificate
the state employee sent didn't belong to Grandma Mary. This
Mary was white. This Mary was born in 1930 and died in 1979.
This Mary was married to a man named Joe Buckley, not John
Buckley. She had parents who were remembered and named on
her certificate of death. This Mary was a nurse, which means
she had the privilege of education, of knowing how to read.
She lived in Bastrop, Louisiana, not DeRidder. She died by
"asphyxiation as a consequence of aspiration of gastric con-
tents." She was buried in a cemetery called Welcome Home.
This Mary has a story, a story that, like everyone's story, war-
rants remembering and telling.

But this Mary was not my Mary.

I had to call the state about the error. But I had to calm
down first. I felt exhausted over something that should not be
this exhausting.

The woman who took my call was all business.

"Please send the incorrect death certificate back immediately," she said. "Now, in order to try to locate the correct one,
we're going to need as much information as possible. Who
were Mary Buckley's parents?"

"You mean, who were my great-grandmother's parents?"

"Yes, we need that kind of information. Where they were born. The exact year . . ."

I laughed, but it did not sound like a laugh.

"I have no idea who her parents were," I said. My voice rose. I was indignant that I was being asked to prove, again and again, the validity of something that was stolen.

"I have no idea when they were born because I have absolutely no idea, no record, no anything of who they were. They were black. I do know that. And, as you know, we don't have a lot of information about many of our black ancestors."

"Yes, yes. I understand," the woman said hurriedly. "We're going to do as much as we can, ma'am."

I let out a breath.

"Thank you," I said.

In this small battle over my ancestors' existence, Louisiana edged out Mississippi once again.

TO SOLOMON

DECEMBER 28, 2006
It may be a boy, Dr. Dwight said. I left his office, went to the restroom, and had a breakdown. What will I do with a boy? I thought. What will Marcus do with a THIRD boy? He was sad, too, but we are better now.

JANUARY 12, 2007
Happy New Year!
This is the first year that I will give birth, a literal birth.

JANUARY 20, 2007
Dear Solomon,
I cannot wait for you to get here, cannot wait to hold you in my arms, to kiss your cheeks, your lips.
It is true: I had dreamed of having a little girl; I had felt the ache of desire in my heart for her, her hair, her precious little fashions. Carmen was to be her name.
Yet I should have known you were inside me. Twice, you visited me in my dreams, pleading with your eyes and anxious smile for me to accept you. I am sorry, son, that I was so blind. I am falling in love with you now, and I have felt you move, a slow grazing under my belly. So strange! So lovely!

You have been moving all day, little man! I believe that is you, anyway.

Your name means "peace." Will you be peaceful? And to think, just last week, I panicked because I really had not felt you move. Marcus and I went to the doctor where, at first, the nurse put the fetal monitor on my belly. Nothing. No heartbeat. This went on for several excruciatingly long minutes—her dragging the monitor across my belly. Finally, the doctor came in and said that it was too early in my pregnancy for that particular machine, so they brought me to the ultrasound room where he saw your heartbeat right away, and then we saw it and breathed sighs of relief. Dr. Dwight said that he was 99 percent sure you're a boy.

You have two brothers by your father's seed: Immanuel, who will be fifteen when you arrive, and Yanni, who will have just turned twelve.

The whole blended family thing is so difficult, and yet it is most prevalent today. I have had a tough time with it, personally, though in reality, it's still early.

MARCH 6, 2007

Dear Solomon,

You just moved—a stronger stirring in my abdomen now; you are so strong. I'm on the floor in what is my office and will double as your baby room, lying under a desk across from your father as he works. I am too tired to work. My fingers cramp just from writing this letter. The ache has radiated upward to my elbows and shoulders.

MARCH 21, 2007

Dear Solomon,

Have you been dreaming? I sure have. I dream crazy dreams, so colorful and vivid. I've dreamed twice these two weeks that my baby was here. In one, you'd come early. In another, I had to give birth to you by myself because no one was available.

APRIL 22, 2007
Pregnancy update:
I am HUGE!

FINDINGS AND LEAVINGS

WHEN MARY'S CORRECT death certificate arrived in the mail, my fingers shook. What revelations would it hold? What omissions and disappointments? My mother didn't seem too keen on the idea of me scratching around for death papers. Her own health was failing, and perhaps my preoccupation with the dead instead of hands-on involvement in the lives of my still-living relatives—namely, her—was unsettling. Perhaps my attempts were even ungodly.

"Paul wrote that squabbling over genealogies is foolish work," she said on a few occasions.

I was too afraid to ask her if she felt that I fell into that category of fools.

I suppose it's strange to call a piece of paper verifying someone's death good news, but it felt substantial; it felt like something. While I can vividly remember pieces of Grandma Mary, flashes, so very many years have passed, decades, and since I was still a child when she died, in some ways, she seems as elusive as an urban myth. No one recorded her voice speaking or singing. I do not know what happened to her braid.

So to see her name in print on an official government document stirred up something warm in me. A validation. I ran my thumb over the silvery state seal, the Louisiana pelican. "I certify that this is a true and correct copy of a certificate or document registered with the Vital Records Registry of the State of Louisiana . . ." the line next to it read, signed by the state registrar.

"True and correct."

The certificate lists her as Mary M. Buckley. Female. Black. Widowed. She was born on April 15, 1890, which would make her only fifteen at the time of her son's birth. She and Burt were young lovers. In those times, though, they were marrying age. For birthplace, only Mississippi is named. Under kind of business or industry she worked in, the word "none" is typed in the blank. She was a "housewife," it documents, although I know that this is not the full story. She was a farmer. An earlier census I found on a website identified her as such, and my mother has told me that she farmed. She tilled the land, and she fed those who were even poorer than she with her harvest. As girls, Dena and I used to help Grandmama Avis cook and can vats of fruits and vegetables, and I wonder now if any of it came from Grandma Mary's land in Old Heights before it was overrun from disuse.

Grandma Mary was a farmer.

A survivor.

A lifeline.

Her social security number is on the form. Also, her date of death, October 13, 1982; place of death and burial (DeRidder); and name of the funeral director, Mr. Vincent (the now-deceased black father of one of my best childhood friends). Papa Houston's signature verifies that the information he provided on his mother is correct to the best of his knowledge. He signed this validation on October 14, 1982.

Mary had died at 7:40 p.m. the night before from a condition that is illegible to my eye but that she is listed as having had for eighteen years between the onset of the condition and her death. She died at a nursing home, Beauregard Parish

Nursing Home. I remember when she left our house and was admitted into the nursing home. I remember the adults talking about her falling and breaking her hip.

I do pray that there is peace and there is rest after death. That there is heaven, although Marcus does not believe in all that. He is an agnostic. While I struggle with doubt from time to time, I am a believer. I pray that there is a heaven for my ancestors' sake. Grandmama prayed forward.

"Lord, protect my children and my children's children and my children's, children's, children," she would pray. "Don't let all this evil come upon them in their day."

I understand why we believe. Our ancestors deserved better than what this earthly home wrought. I only wish that I could have prayed backward for their lives here.

Mary.

There was good news in this death certificate. For the first time, I learned the names of her parents—my great-great-grandparents. The certificate says that her father was Fate McGee (though Papa Houston may have spelled it incorrectly) and her mother was Martha Sarton (maiden name). Later, on a census reporter, I found a "Martha Sartin" instead of "Martha Sarton." Next to their names are their places of birth, both listed as Holmesville, Mississippi. I was beside myself. I carried the paper like a delicate leaf to the kitchen where Marcus was washing dishes. I held it out to him. He looked down at the navy-blue-framed lilac sheet of paper shaking in my fingers.

"What is it?" he asked.

"It's them. I found them."

"Found who?"

"My family. Grandma Mary. Her parents! I found them!"

"Oh wow, that's great, babe," he said and hugged me, suds dripping to the floor. He pulled back. "Look at you, finding your people." Then he paused. "You know, it makes me wonder who my people were."

"Isn't it crazy," I said, "going through life not knowing who you're connected to, where they came from? It makes you desperate, I think. Makes you want to make shit up."

"I think my pops' folks are from Louisiana, but I don't know who they were."

"Uh-oh, we could be cousins," I said. We laughed and shook our heads. Marcus turned back to the sink.

"Fucking US of A," I said.

"Yeah, it's fucked up all right."

ONE MORNING DURING my pregnancy, as I was cleaning out an armoire Marcus had given me to house my journals, paperwork, and old newspaper clippings, I came across a journal entry that I wrote in 2003 while Ric and I were still together:

> *New forms struggle to emerge, but I've got one foot stuck in the past. How can I reproduce? My child would come here weighed down with the unresolved past, this thing that sits stubbornly in the middle of me. Inertia. Sterility. A fetus cannot form in the midst of century-old decay. That is as far as my body can remember. My intestines and ovaries are corroded with this memory. My body is not equipped to hold a baby. How would I stomach it? And from where would the umbilical cord form? A century ago, it was left wrapped around a tree.*

I do not remember writing this. What else do I not remember? Or misremember? How long had I wanted a child before I knew I wanted a child? I had moved to California with thoughts of freedom dangling in my mind, having long ago declared that I would never give birth, but did my body already know that it was on its way to becoming a mother and, somehow, was psychologically preparing? And if that is so, who or what was in control of my body? I regarded myself as independent and quietly rebellious. After some initial pestering from outsiders about how I "needed" to become a mother, no one was demanding this of me anymore—no one from the living, conscious realm. Likewise, while I had Uncle Cricket's blessings to write a book exploring our family's past, the onus was on me—one that carried me into the underworld of uncovering my psychological need to get at the root of family questions I'd been largely able to ignore while still living in Louisiana.

I was excited to forge my own path in the West, yet choosing to conceive, to ultimately walk in my foremothers' shoes, was, perhaps, my way of creating a foundation for myself as I uprooted.

WHEN I TOLD Ric that I was pregnant, he was happy for me. We shared a vegan hot dog lunch and listened to the changes in each other's lives.

"Do you think I'm crazy?" I asked him. "Getting pregnant after all we went through. Being with this guy. He's pushing forty, already has big kids, and they are not at all excited to see me in their father's life."

"They'll come around," Ric said. "And no, I don't think you're crazy." He drizzled ketchup over his fries. "I always knew you'd make a wonderful mother. I often wondered if you secretly wished you'd made another decision."

"Wow, you did? Honestly, it never became a desire of mine until after I started teaching. Something strange just started happening in my mind, in my body—I don't know." Tears sprung before I could tamper them. "But, Ric, I'm so sorry about what I did to you."

"Look, Sand . . . I want you to be happy. It's unfortunate how things happened, but you can still be happy." We ate in silence for a while.

"I've finally got enough money saved up to leave the country," he said.

"Oh my God, Ric—that's wonderful."

"I'm going to Lima, Peru, first, but I don't plan to stay anywhere for long. At some point, I will land in Africa. I want to document the lives of marginalized people in as many places as I can."

"This is what you have always wanted," I said. "I'm so happy for you."

And I was. But I also felt my heart sinking. I am losing a friend, I thought. My best friend. Our marriage had brought us to Los Angeles, and now Ric was preparing to leave while I would stay and face an uncertain future as a mom, as a stepmom, and as someone else's mate.

PROTECTIVE INSTINCTS

THERE WAS LIKELY no need for what we in the black community call "the Talk" during the days when Burt and Mary were growing up.

When you are born into that kind of in-your-face oppression, when the line between black and white, what's yours and what's theirs, where you can go and where you dare not venture, whom you can be with, and whom you'd better not be caught dead with, the Talk is not in the least bit necessary.

Before he had language, Burt had drunk the Talk for breast milk and then later eaten it as mushed-up food for breakfast, lunch, supper, and dinner. He saw the Talk in his father's slumped shoulders and his mother's downcast eyes whenever he went with her into town and a white person walked by or when the overseer, with his tall yellow teeth, came to collect all the family's hard earnings. He saw it in the way his mother's nostrils spread whenever that overseer spit on the side of her porch, projecting his spittle onto the leaves of her roses, something sweet and living. He might as well have spat onto her face because, in essence, he did. Low-down dirty old rascal, his mother's eyes hissed, and if looks could kill . . . so she didn't meet his eyes.

"Like he couldn't wait until he got on down the got-damned road," his mother would say once the white man was out of earshot. She would say "got" because she'd taught him not to swear—"don't take the Lord's name in vain"—but to say "damned road" all by itself just didn't cut it, so she compromised. And it would have been one thing if the man had spat on her roses once, or even twice, but the fact was, he did it every single time.

Those small moments were kicks to the stomach, hammering out his family's place in the world.

All of those moments were part of the battle for their livelihoods, their very souls, and as a kid growing up in those times, you understood this almost from infancy because a baby breathes in the air of his time, and just as you do not walk around marveling at the existence of air, as a parent raising children in that kind of oppressiveness, you do not waste your breath on the obvious.

Until you realize, too late, that maybe you should have— that maybe there was something you could have done to save your son's, or your daughter's, life.

As I prepared my birth plan, I wondered when Marcus and I would have to have the Talk with Solomon. How long would we have before another child ostracized him because of his color? How old would he be before he is profiled by the police? An expectant mother should not have to think that far ahead. An expectant mother should not have to conjure a death-prevention plan as she writes out her birth plan.

TRYING TO GET in some final workouts before the baby, I went on a lone hike at Griffith Park one evening, but I miscalculated the timing of the setting sun. It was near twilight as I made my way back down the hill. As I turned a bend, a coyote was standing on my path, the well-traveled path. I stopped, my sneakers kicking up a half-cloud of dust. The coyote watched me watch him. He looked at me as though I were a curious thing, as though my presence surprised him as much as his surprised me. "What are you doing up here at this time, human?" He inched toward me. I looked around, but we were alone.

"Okay, buddy, you can have the big path," I whispered. "I'll find another way." I walked to the edge of a cliff where a steep, narrow trail had been carved by the more adventurous. Had there been more light, I would have naturally chosen this route, but I had not worn hiking boots, so I knew my grip going down the stark path would be slippery. And with my huge belly, I was already at a disadvantage as my sense of balance, having never been optimal, was at an all-time low. My intestines fluttered. I turned my body sideways and descended, stepping gingerly but solidly, the way Ric had shown me when we first moved to LA. A lover of thrills and risks, he nevertheless approached such activities with preparation, caution, and, if lucky enough to have a pupil, detailed instructions. With his voice in my head, I crouched a little and began to inch my way down ("you want to be close to the ground if you fall," Ric would say), but my belly was heavy and in the way. It was suddenly dark. As I squinted, I thought I could make out flat land. I was near the bottom of the hill. My feet slipped on loose gravel, and I hit the dirt with a thud and rolled down the rest of the hill. When I stopped, I brought both hands to my stomach. The baby was still. My heart *thumped, thumped, thumped*. My elbows and the side of my face stung, but I knew my scars were just on the surface. I stayed on the ground, imagining the coyote watching me from his vantage point at the top of the hill.

Then I felt a long, sluggish movement dragging underneath my belly. The baby was okay; he was fine. I covered my face with my hands and laughed there in the dark with the earth.

A CROSSING

MAY 9, 2007

I am thirty-five weeks pregnant. The pain in my pelvic area is unbearable. I'm not sure what it means, but I see the doctor tomorrow. He says he wants me to stay off my feet as much as possible. For now, I am still working. At school, our first newspaper, the Knightly News, *came out yesterday, produced by my students and me. The school's first paper. How exciting!*

MAY 18, 2007

At my checkup today, a woman named Carolina took my blood pressure. Later, I read that the baby will need eight to twelve feedings a day, will have six to eight wet diapers, and should have at least two bowel movements. It all sounds like so much!

MAY 26, 2007

I am home alone. My feet and ankles are swollen as big as an elephant's. The doctor has ordered me off my feet, so I had to leave my students before the semester ended.

My labor is a couple of weeks away, but I am hoping it comes sooner. My cervix is soft and anterior but still had not, as of yesterday, opened at all.

MAY 30, 2007

I smell of sweat and overripe fruit. Inside my body live both my dead ancestors and my unborn offspring. It is the decision to give birth— that process of carrying and delivering my child—that connects me to my past. My body is a river, a channel. With Solomon's birth, Burt will live again, breathe again.

IN THE HOURS before giving birth, I know with pure certainty that I am going to die. Not from the pain but from a frost that starts in the marrow of my bones and crawls its way into every internal organ and out to my skin. I prepare my mind to say goodbye to my body.

I had wanted to have the baby naturally. Like everything else, I had romanticized his birth and wanted to, in alignment with a beautiful YouTube video I had seen and the books I had read, allow the baby to slip out of me and into a pool of warm water. But my little circle of water, that sack that acted as a protective shield between my baby and the rest of me and, therefore, the world and all of its contagions, broke at midnight (I was sitting on the living room sofa watching a comedy show), but I tried to keep my cool since the contractions were still spaced pretty far apart.

Marcus and I had rushed to the hospital a week earlier. It was a false alarm.

"I can hold out," I told Marcus after my water broke, and we eventually went to bed where I would drift off until a contraction hit me with enough force to make me sit straight up, gritting my teeth until it subsided. I had to pee even more than usual, so I kept rolling my body out of bed and ambling down the hallway.

We went to the hospital around 5:30 a.m. It was a Sunday, June 3. I was not dilated much at all, but the doctor said he would not be able to follow my birth plan.

"The risk for infection is too great," he explained.

I did not fight him. Deflated, I lumbered over to the bed as Marcus cupped my elbow.

"I can still have him naturally at least," I said.

"Yes, of course," Dr. Dwight said. "I will see you when you are ready to deliver."

"Wait. Where are you going?"

"Back home."

"Home?

"Just relax. You haven't dilated much at all. The nurses will call me when it's time, and I'll be right here."

About eight hours in, I had the nurse call the doctor. She gave me the receiver. I was sobbing so hard he could barely understand me.

"Look, honey, it's okay to take the epidural," Dr. Dwight said.

"But I tried so hard," I said feeling broken.

"Girlfriend, if I were a woman, I'd take the meds."

I called my mother next. She wouldn't be in Los Angeles for another seven days, having scheduled her flight based on the doctor's predicted delivery date.

"I failed, Mama," I said. "All the research says it's better for the babies if you have them naturally, but I can't take it anymore."

"I don't know about all that research," she said. "But I do know that after having you and Dena the so-called natural way, every time I had a baby after that, I told the doctor, 'Give me my shot.'"

As they prepped me for the epidural, I could not erase the vision of a long silver needle being inserted into my spine. My mother had told Dena and me about this procedure when we were growing up.

"And you can't move an inch," she said once. "You have to

stay very still so that they can insert the needle. If they do it wrong, you can become paralyzed."

I was sitting on the edge of Mama's bed that day. My spine felt as though it were shriveling. I drew my shoulders to my neck and shuddered.

Mama laughed.

"Girl, you can't stand to hear nothing about the body, can you? You can't hear talk about giving birth, and now you can't hear about a needle going in your back."

"I can't take that kind of stuff," I said, still cringing. I wonder now if her "talks" were a form of birth control for her daughters.

"You have to be very still," my anesthesiologist said. He was sitting on the edge of my bed after giving me the medical rundown of how the epidural would be inserted and what I could expect in terms of pain relief.

"Be very still," he said again, softly. My back was exposed to him, and I felt unspeakably vulnerable. He wiped my back down with something cold and numbing. I squeezed my eyes tight and tried to will my shaking body still, but the more I tried to stop the trembling, the more it overtook me. As the needle went in and then withdrew, the shaking grew worse. I became cold, freezing cold, and it seemed to take form in the marrow of my bones. Someone, my nurse perhaps, pushed me onto my back and covered me with blankets. Blankets that I could not feel.

This is it, I thought. This is death. I closed my eyes. I was ready. But the thoughts kept coming, and I wondered, Does the mind live on even after death? With each blanket they piled on top of me, I imagined the horror of someone thought dead but alive being buried, counting each shovelful of dirt and unable to open her eyes or her mouth.

I heard Marcus ask the nurse for extra pillows. "I'm just going to lie down on this sofa for a bit," he said.

I wanted to yell at him. Why are you lying down? Can't you see that I am dying? And where is the music that I said I wanted to play? Wait—is that music I hear? It sounds so far away. I cannot tell.

I WOKE WITH my nurse and Marcus standing over me. Someone had propped up my upper body. Everything was numb, heavy, and hazy. I peered through the fog at something bright in the distance heading toward me.

It was Dr. Dwight clad in a blue-and-white Hawaiian shirt; he was chirpy and refreshed.

"Are we ready?" he asked, his voice an ocean breeze. He looked between my legs.

"Ha! I see the head!" he shrieked as though it was the first emerging head he had ever seen.

I was hopeful with him looking like that and sounding like that. I thought, If he sees the head, I am almost done. I am going to be one of those women who will say, "The next thing I knew, the baby was in my arms. I hardly felt a thing."

The birthing of my baby did not turn out like that.

He was, in a word, stuck.

"Cassandra, you're going to have to push, baby, push," Dr. Dwight said.

Marcus said, "Breathe. Push. Remember?" He held my hand. It was supposed to be warm and reassuring, but the medicine made it impossible to feel any of that.

I took short breaths the way the birthing class instructor had shown us. Marcus mirrored me. "It's just so different from how they said," I said. "Everything is so . . . different."

I believed I was pushing, but I couldn't be sure. I worried

that I wouldn't be able to push my baby out of me, but I was especially afraid of the afterbirth. I was convinced that little pieces of the placenta and fetal membranes would remain inside me—floating around, unable to find an opening. Would it be dead or alive? Remnants of the past, the future, or both?

My lower torso felt a world apart from the rest of me, and yet the pain was incomparable to anything I'd ever felt. I was in a state of suspension—there was no beginning and there was no end. I was stuck in the middle of a bridge that felt impossible to cross. The folks at my feet were rescuers down on the ground below the other side of this bridge I was suspended on, a bridge they all knew was about to blow, except no one could say exactly when. I saw myself on the edge of this bridge, with my head swelling with fear, with people on the other side telling me to "Jump! Just jump!" as though this was the easiest thing in the world to do, but it was not because all of a sudden, I was deathly afraid of heights and a swell of vertigo was pulling me back, back away from these people. They told me that there were soft nets to catch me, but I could not go on, and I stopped even wanting whatever they were offering.

In the end, I could not remain where I was, and the reality and impossibility of these two contradictions engulfed me with dread and the realization that no one could do this thing for me. I was on my own. And stuck between my womb and the threshold of this world was a new generation for which I would be responsible: a black boy. I needed my mother. I needed all the women of my southern childhood to guide me through the delivery and its aftermath, but they were not there, and their absence bore down on me, threatening to rip me apart.

Eventually, I sensed a shift. Something lifting me and nature and gravity as one. Inside I called upon my foremothers—"Mama, Grandmama, Grandma Mary"—and pushed as though our lives depended on it.

WHEN THE BABY and I finished our struggle of pushing away and into and out of each other, Dr. Dwight grabbed him. He held him up like a trophy, a shining yellow-pink creature with a wet mass of curls matted against his soft head.

"What a beautiful baby," Dr. Dwight said.

Solomon was silent and alert with an alarming clarity. Marcus cut the cord. The nurse wiped the baby gently and then laid him belly down on my chest. A river of blue ran through his skin.

He lifted his head and stared, clear-eyed, into my eyes.

"Oh my God, he's looking dead at me!" I screamed. "Hello, my son. You are so beautiful!"

Something warm spread over my belly. A liquid blanket.

I gasped.

"He . . . he's peeing on me!"

Everyone laughed, and I laughed too.

"You did it, baby," Marcus said. He kissed my forehead, my cheeks, and my lips.

"I did it," I said, hearing my own voice sound like a little girl's. I looked at Marcus. "We did it."

"Who . . . this guy?" Dr. Dwight said. "All he had to do is use a pair of scissors. His job was easy."

Marcus's mother and brother, followed by Yanni, his eyes filled with a shy excitement, filed into the room after I breast-fed Solomon. They fawned over the baby, and I tried to keep my eyes open for their visit. When visiting time was over and the nurse whisked the baby away for testing, Marcus kissed me good-night. I fell into a deep sleep with my gown baptized in my baby's clear and odorless urine.

BLACK FUTURES

"COME, COME, CHILD," Leola beckons, holding her small hand out to Mary.

Mary places her palm into the older woman's. It is warm and strong. Leola pulls her to the back of the room. She opens a wooden door and it groans, widening to reveal a black room thick with the scent of pine. Mary's pupils expand and contract as they adjust to the darkness. She realizes the room is not completely devoid of light. A couple of candles burn from shelves nailed into the walls. Mary looks deeper. Some of the wall panels are made of tin and some of wood. Tiny pinholes in the tin panels let in dots of daylight like little stars punctuating the darkness. Squares of colorful cloth hang down from the ceiling like chandeliers.

Leola leads Mary to a chair and coaxes her to lean her head back over a tin washtub that sits atop a stack of cinder blocks. She dips a cup into the tub and pours water, slowly, slowly, over Mary's head. It is warm and thick as molasses coating Mary's scalp.

"Let go, child," Leola whispers, and Mary inhales air the size of a whale. She lets it go, and this letting go hollows her out until she feels small, like a wisp of a thing, like a girl, under Leola's magical hands and a river of water pushing its bright fragrance through the air, cutting through the darkness, and dancing across notes of pine.

"Leola," Mary says, startled. "What is that smell?"

"Orange blossoms," Leola answers.

"I don't know it," Mary says. "Don't believe I smelled the flowers of oranges before."

Leola chuckles. "Why should you have? Ain't no orange trees nowhere 'round here."

"Where'd you get it, then?"

"From my travels," Leola says mysteriously.

Laughter gurgles in Mary's stretched-back throat. "Travels! Leola, where you been?"

"That's for me to know and you to find out. Maybe I been to Mobile, Mexico, Jupiter, the moon." She laughs. "Or maybe, I been to the future."

"The future? The future, Leola? What is the future?" Mary turns her head slightly under the water. "Leola, you funny. What in the world do you mean—the future?"

But Leola doesn't answer. She is done talking. Her fingers massage the perfumed water into Mary's hair; they press against every inch of her scalp until Mary's eyes close—dark against dark—until her neck is limp and her head is light. Leola's fingers press and press and press, emptying Mary's head of all its knots of tension and underneath that all of its questions until she, too, has no more words.

ACKNOWLEDGMENTS

I HAVE BEEN picking at this book for so long it feels like a whole human being. Thanks to God for breath, for beauty, for all the flesh-and-blood humans who tolerated me as I pieced this story together over the years—dreaming and fretting and sequestering myself away. Bottomless thank-yous to my siblings: Lydia, Andrea, Nicholas, Dane, and Kendrick. I believe in all of you and am blessed by your individual brilliance. So much love to Mama (Pamela Coar). Your words and strings have shaped me in ways you cannot know. And thank you, George Coar, for your love and support.

To my cousins and aunts-in-law: love you! Irwin Thompson: thank you for showing me what was possible, for leading the way. Thank you to Avia Perry for the title inspiration, and Mama Sunshine for inspiring the final scene.

To my ancestors: because you were, we are, and I will always hold your names in my heart. To put them down in ink is an utmost honor. A special memorial to Uncle Cricket for pushing me to write and finish this book. I have been carrying the weight of letting you down, but even in death, you are teaching me about the power of forgiveness.

Words cannot express how absolutely thrilled I still am to get to work with the extraordinary Feminist Press team: publisher and executive director Jamia Wilson (you inspire me beyond words!), senior editor Lauren Rosemary Hook and assistant editor Nick Whitney (you are gifted and superb editors), as well as Jisu Kim, Rachel Page, and Lucia Brown—all of you have made this experience the absolute highlight of my creative and professional career. A million thank-yous to Krystal Quiles for her gorgeous cover design. It was a delight to win the 2020 Louise Meriwether First Book Prize, named in honor of a woman whose work I deeply admire. Additional gratitude to *TAYO Literary Magazine* and all the esteemed judges.

As for the earlier writing journey, there are too many people to name. Martha Lou Roberts: thank you for two years of kick-butt literature and composition, and for encouraging me all these years later. Boundless gratitude to Kalamu ya Salaam, my first true writing mentor, and all of the wonderful writers and poets who made up NOMMO Literary Society, as well as to the amazing Community Book Center in New Orleans. You opened my eyes to what was possible in language, what is possible for Black writers, what it means to be in community. I am forever grateful to the late great Harold Battiste; to my big sis of the heart, Vera Johnson; and to the extraordinary writers Tameka Cage Conley (my Louisiana sis), Yona Harvey, Jericho Brown, and Terrance Hayes. You stand in your power as literary artists and I have always been in awe of you.

Moving to Los Angeles: a huge thank-you to all of my writing mentors and friends (and all of Antioch University's MFA program), particularly Nana-Ama Danquah (so many thanks to you and Greg Tate for publishing the first seeds of this!), Brenda Miller, and Bernadette Murphy. I am forever indebted to s.t.a.r.s. workshop, founded by my dear friend Kaaren Kitchell, for all the great feedback during this manuscript's baby stages. What you and Richard Beban (miss him so much!) created for artists and writers over the years is immeasurable. All my love to you—and to Jennifer Genest, John Truby, Jon Hess,

Anna Waterhouse, Dawna Kemper, and Diane Sherry Case. Deep gratitude to the writers who helped this book through its adolescent phase: Ryane Nicole Granados, LaCoya Katoe Gessessee, Ramona Wright, Jennifer (again), Tisha Marie Reichle-Aguilera, Amanda Hollander. Thank you for your eyes and hearts as well Tanya Ko Hong, Krishna Buford, Darlene Taylor, Breena Clarke, Cheryl Clarke, Gerda Govine, Mike Sonksen, Peggy Dobreer, Sharon Rapport, Charu Saxena, and Stuart Balcomb. An unending heart of gratitude to the dynamos behind and a part of *Ms. Aligned*, *Fury*, *Everything But the Burden*, AROHO, VONA, Raising Mothers, *Writers Resist*, RoarShack, Library Girl, Beyond Baroque, and Women Who Submit. A special thank-you to poet and writing career coach Li Yun Alvarado. Debra Monroe: you are likely sick of my gushes of thanks, but thank you for your brilliance, for helping guide this book in a huge way, and especially for new friendship. Huge gratitude to my New Life LA family and all fitness friends: Thank you for working my body, mind, and spirit! All of it sustains and uplifts.

So much love to the mega-talented Dayna Lynne North for her support and love—and for introducing me to a group of Black women powerhouses in LA twenty years ago, the Chai Bellas, founded by the phenomenal Nichelle Protho. You ladies are my superheroes. More heroes: Lolis Eric Elie and Lynell George. Thank you for your stellar work as writers and for your friendship.

Thank you to past and current employers and colleagues and so many heart blessings to all my former students!

Thank you, Black Lives Matter, and all who are fighting to save our lives and ensure we not only survive but thrive.

Ric Francis: Thank you for your support over all these years, for your forgiveness and love. You have a friend in me. Always.

Yanni and Immanuel: I am proud of you and I love you. You are young, gifted, and Black and beautiful. Stand in that power. So much love and gratitude to Charmaine and Mesan Richardson!

And finally: eternal galaxies of love and appreciation to my husband and son, Marcus and Solomon Rich. Thank you for your unending support, for all the ways you challenge me to keep growing, and for allowing me to be myself. My heart is threaded with yours.

PHOTO © DANIEL RARELA

CASSANDRA LANE is a writer and editor based in Los Angeles. Lane received her MFA from Antioch University LA. Her stories have appeared in the *New York Times*'s Conception series, the *Times-Picayune*, the *Atlanta-Journal Constitution*, and elsewhere. She is managing editor of *L.A. Parent* magazine and formerly served on the board of the AROHO Foundation.

More Nonfiction from the Feminist Press

Against Memoir: Complaints, Confessions & Criticisms
by Michelle Tea

Black Dove: Mamá, Mi'jo, and Me
by Ana Castillo

Fault Lines
by Meena Alexander

I Had a Miscarriage: A Memoir, a Movement
by Jessica Zucker

Knitting the Fog
by Claudia D. Hernández

A Life in Motion
by Florence Howe

The Names of All the Flowers
by Melissa Valentine

The Raging Skillet: The True Life Story of Chef Rossi
by Rossi

Still Alive: A Holocaust Girlhood Remembered
by Ruth Kluger

Tenemental: Confessions of a Reluctant Landlady
by Vikki Warner

Translation as Transhumance
by Mireille Gansel, translated by Ros Schwartz

The Feminist Press publishes books that ignite movements and social transformation. Celebrating our legacy, we lift up insurgent and marginalized voices from around the world to build a more just future.

See our complete list of books at
feministpress.org

Founded in 2016, **The Louise Meriwether First Book Prize** is awarded to a debut work by a woman or nonbinary author of color in celebration of the legacy of Louise Meriwether. Presented by the Feminist Press in partnership with *TAYO Literary Magazine*, the prize seeks to uplift much-needed stories that shift culture and inspire a new generation of writers.

**THE LOUISE MERIWETHER
FIRST BOOK PRIZE**

THE FEMINIST PRESS
AT THE CITY UNIVERSITY OF NEW YORK
FEMINISTPRESS.ORG